The Book of

THE
PARTY
ANIMAL

The Book of
◆ THE ◆
PARTY ANIMAL

A Champion's Guide to
PARTY SKILLS, PRANKS, AND MAYHEM

by **BEN APPLEBAUM & DAN DISORBO**
Foreword by Andrew W. K.

CHRONICLE BOOKS
SAN FRANCISCO

Library of Congress Cataloging-in-Publication Data:

Applebaum, Ben, author.

The Book of the party animal: a champion's guide to party skills, pranks, and mayhem / by Ben Applebaum and Dan DiSorbo; illustrations by Dan DiSorbo; foreword by Andrew W. K.

pages cm

ISBN 978-1-4521-1885-7

1. Parties—Humor. I. DiSorbo, Dan, illustrator. II. Title.

PN6231.P32A66 2013

818'.602—dc23

2012049258

Manufactured in China.

Designed by Real Art Design Group.

10 9 8 7 6 5 4 3 2 1

Chronicle Books, LLC

680 Second Street

San Francisco, California 94107

www.chroniclebooks.com

"Carpe Noctem"

PARTY ANIMALS ARE FUN AND SOCIAL CREATURES who *should* party responsibly and in moderation. And while partying oftentimes involves drinking alcohol, underage drinking is something we don't condone and never support.

The material contained in this book is presented only for informational and amusement purposes only. The publisher and authors do not condone or advocate in any way the use of prohibited substances or the excessive consumption of alcohol, underage drinking, underage tobacco use, and we accept no liability for the consequences of unlawful drinking, overindulgence, or illegal activity of any kind.

If you decide to drink, drink responsibly, know your limits, never drink and drive, and never let your buddies drink and drive. Use a designated driver system, call a cab, take public transportation, or sleep it off. Just don't get behind the wheel.

Please Party Responsibly!

Table of Awesomeness

HELLO! *My name is Andrew W.K. and I love to party. I love it so much that fifteen years ago I decided to make it my life's calling. I'm proud to say that I'm now a professional partier and that partying has made all my dreams come true.*

But it wasn't always easy—it took dedication, extreme effort, and many hours of studying and learning this special art form. I believe that partiers are both born and made, which is good news if you're someone who wants to become a true Party Animal but haven't yet taken the plunge. It's never too late to increase the amount of party in your life, and even if you don't go professional with it, a stronger commitment to joy and celebration can only improve your experience.

The further we journey through this adventure of not being dead, the more we have to be grateful for and celebrate. Partying helps us appreciate the good in our lives. It's basically impossible to be in a state of gratitude and a bad mood at the same time. Partying feeds our souls and helps us remember the vast amount of possibility and excitement that life has to offer. It helps us avoid the pitfalls of complacency, depression, logic, and rational behavior.

That's why I've always looked at partying as an "all-the-time-thing." Lots of people told me you're only supposed to party on the weekend, when you're glad it's Friday. Or on holidays, New Year's, or when you celebrate the start of something new. If partying is recognizing and heralding what you're grateful for, why can't you celebrate being alive every day? We're grateful to not be dead! That is the art of the party mindset!

Unfortunately, there have been many organizations that believe partying is bad. They want a world of stiff limits and a sense of order and correctness that can ultimately crush the human spirit and exterminate all the Party Animals on this great planet. I've made it my mission to see that this never happens, and the fact that you're reading this book is a sign that hopefully you will join this cause as well. Not only is it important that we fight to save Party Animals from extinction, but it's equally important that we encourage and develop the Party Animal inside each of us. A partier life is a better life, and it's what makes the human being the awesomest animal of all.

The desire to be happy, cheerful, joyful, crazy, and awash in orgasmic chaos is part of the vibrant fabric of the human spirit. It's what bonds us to one another, to our own soul, and to the universal positive power of existence. I've learned more about myself through having fun than by any amount of dry soul-searching. When we party, we dive into life—we get wet and bring out the best we have to offer this world. Our joy spreads through the cosmos and multiplies. In that way, it's our obligation to celebrate the life we've been given, and make the most of this miracle called reality. Enjoy this book and become the best Party Animal you can be.

Party Hard Forever!

Your friend,
ANDREW W.K.
The King of Partying

Introduction

THE NORTH AMERICAN
PARTY ANIMAL IS ENDANGERED.

---◆---

Today's world is dominated more by social networks than by socializing. Friends are added and subtracted with the click of a button. And chatting happens over the computer instead of over a drink.

Today's world is neutered. A night is deemed a success if a few laughs escape from the miasma of pleasantries and moderation. Wild abandon has been replaced by domesticated chitchat.

Today's world needs Party Animals like never before. But who will mentor the next generation of maniacs? Who will coach the future carousers? Who will help the next freak flags fly?

You, that's who.

You have the ability—dare we say, obligation?—to keep the Party Animal flame alive.

To that end, we have taken the collective experience of the greatest hell-raisers of all time and distilled it into this powerful, proven guide. From ancient bacchanalian Greeks to the suburbanites donning lampshades to the rock stars who party like, well, rock stars, Party Animals have left their mark on history—and the carpet.

Now it's time to leave yours. It's time to celebrate, protect, and encourage the proliferation of the North American Party Animal. To help you better master the complexity of the Party Animal's instincts and abilities, we've created a simple acronym (P-A-R-T-Y) to help you understand the basics of what it takes to be a champion Party Animal.

P = PREPARE The first step to partying actually happens well before the partying begins. A Party Animal must be properly educated, rested, well-hydrated, and well-fed. We will discuss this further in Chapters 1 and 2.

A = ADAPT Knowing the party scene is half the battle, and owning the party is the other half. From house parties and toga parties to foam parties and after parties, Party Animals must be able to adapt and acclimate to every changing environment including their own home bases, and we've got you covered in Chapter 3.

R = RELATE Party Animals are social creatures through and through. So knowing how to behave and how to interact with one's pack are critical for a Party Animal's survival—at least survival of the night. And Chapters 4 and 5 will cover all the basics.

T = TROUBLE Believe it or not, a Party Animal does have limits. But to find them, he needs to push against them. Sometimes that means rebelling against societal norms. Sometimes that means putting frozen pee under someone's door. Regardless of the manifestation, there is a need for Party Animals to stir up some trouble—and Chapter 6 will help show you how.

Y = YEAH!!! Language is what separates humans from the animals. With the exception being Party Animals who speak in their own language—a lexicon filled with terms for everything from half-drunk beers to half-drunk people. Chapter 7 is your source for how to speak fluent Party Animalese.

CHAPTER

· · 1 · ·

The Party Animal Kingdom

TAXONOMY OF A WILD SPECIES

THE PARTY ANIMAL REPRESENTS one of the greatest products of natural selection in our human evolution. It has evolved throughout the generations to become what some may call a higher life form. (And occasionally, a very high life form.)

In order to fully develop into Party Animals, we must unlock our DNA's inner party chromosome and let it rock out with its genetic code out. To do so, we first need to understand the history, characteristics, evolution, and taxonomy of the Party Animal Kingdom.

This knowledge is not only imperative to preserving the entire species, but also to the Party Animal's ability to adapt and co-evolve in our ever-changing world. "Only the Strong Survive" isn't just a song by Elvis Presley but a way of life.

Think of this chapter as your stretching warm-up before the big game—partying hard. And for those of you about to enter the Party Animal Kingdom, we salute you.

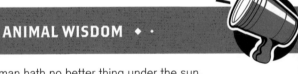

· ◆ ANIMAL WISDOM ◆ ·

"A man hath no better thing under the sun,
than to eat, and to drink, and to be merry."
—*Ecclesiastes 8:15*

Definition of Party Animal

THERE ARE MANY MISCONCEPTIONS and prejudices toward our beloved Party Animal. So let's clear the air, turn up the music, and define exactly what a Party Animal is and, perhaps more importantly, what it is not.

WHAT IS A PARTY ANIMAL?

In order to understand exactly what a Party Animal is, we must first dissect exactly what defines a Party and then an Animal.

The word *party* is derived from the Latin *partire*, which means "to share." It can be used as both a noun and a verb, so it's not just something you attend but something you do. And in the eyes of a Party Animal, party is even more: It's a way of life. And, dare we say, even a perspective on the world.

So for our purposes we can define party as the act of enjoying oneself in a boisterous manner in order to encourage and share good times.

Animal, derived from the Latin *animalis*, meaning "having breath," in its basic form simply means a living organism. But a cooler definition is a beast, a monster, and a savage with instinctive and physical needs.

So when we pair the two words together, we can sum up with a definition like this: a savage beast with an insatiable instinct, internal fortitude, and a desire to enjoy itself in a boisterous manner in order to encourage and share good times. An organism that literally lives and breathes party. And there you have the Party Animal.

THE SEVEN CRITICAL TRAITS OF PARTY ANIMALITY

There are several key traits that differentiate a Party Animal from your average social butterfly. Not to be confused with the seven deadly sins, these seven traits are the top attributes that separate the people who simply like to party from the people who are party incarnate.

1. Extreme extroversion • Party Animals are the life of the party. And, while being the outgoing center-of-attention, standing on the table leading everyone in a drunken chorus of "Sweet Caroline" isn't the only way to demonstrate your extroversion, it is one of the cooler ways.

2. Energy elevation • There is only one direction for a true Party Animal. And that is up. Party Animals bring a palpable energy to every occasion. People can feel it when they walk into the room. They also have to clean it up after the Party Animal walks out.

3. Moderate disregard for authority • Hate "the man" too much and you'll be the Party Animal of cellblock 23C. But get in too close with the powers that be, and you'll be unable to fully rock against something bigger. So a Party Animal must always fight the good fight—without throwing too many haymakers.

4. Animal magnetism • There's a certain something about legendary Party Animals. They possess an inherent leadership ability as well as a charismatic charm that pulls people into their gravitational field.

5. Present in the moment • Party Animals are fully engaged and aware of the "now." While other species spend their days worrying about tomorrow or reliving the past, the Party Animal is ever present—like a Budweiser Buddhist.

6. Down for anything • In a world of "No," Party Animals are a breath of "Yes" air. An impromptu road trip to Vegas? A night out to celebrate a break-up? A strange urge to kidnap a pine tree? Ask a Party Animal and you already know the answer.

7. Relationship lubricator • Interview any group of friends. What you'll find is that the stories they share—the very essence of their bond—was sparked by the Party Animal's role as the Party Catalyst. (Or the Partalyst, as we like to say because we just made it up).

History of the Party Animal •

THOUGH HE'S AT THE APEX OF EVOLUTION, today's North American Party Animal is far from being the first of his kind. Instead, he actually owes much of his existence (and hangover) to generations of raging partiers before him.

Let's take a brief look at the history of the Party Animal: where he's been, what he's drunk, and how he ended up passed out on top of your car.

Down Side of Mr. Good Time

Not everyone loves a Party Animal. At least not all of the time. Here are some of the most common bugaboos about—and our rebuttals.

"TOO CHAOTIC" You can't plan greatness. Sorry Chaz.

"EXHAUSTING" Sleep is for the week—and the weak.

"DANGEROUS" Ships are safer in the harbor, but that's not what ships are for.

"ON ALL THE F'ING TIME" Awesome has no off switch.

"THEY'LL RUIN MY FUTURE POLITICAL ASPIRATIONS"

Okay, good point. Duly noted.

Party Animal	VS	Social Butterfly	VS	Social Networker
• Boisterous		• Obnoxious		• Nosey
• Mingles		• Gossips		• Trolls
• Leader		• Clinger		• Stalker
• Defends friends		• Makes friends		• Collects "friends"
• Loves to party		• Loves attention		• "Likes" anything
• Rally cries		• Whispers secrets		• Instant messages
• Unpredictable		• Restrained		• Removed

2,500,000 B.C. • Neanderthal man kicks off the Party Animal era by actually being half animal.

2,500 B.C. • Pharaoh Djoser builds the first pyramid and suggests, "You guys can totally crash here tonight if you want."

500 B.C. • In Ancient Greece, togas are invented as are some sick drinking games—all before a bunch of boring philosophers began talking.

416 B.C. • The Symposium takes place in Greece, inviting the world's best and brightest philosophers. But when the wine is served, it turns into the biggest game of Thumper in recorded history.

27 B.C. • Caesar is stabbed by Brutus in what is considered one of history's greatest party fouls.

A.D. 406 • Barbarians, the original party crashers, begin invading Western Europe by sacking villages, stealing women, and taking over Beer Pong tables without putting their names on the list.

1059 • Pope Innocent III becomes ruler as the Papal Monarchy takes over. All parties and festivals are required by law to give the Pope a house cup.

1440 • During the Renaissance, Johannes Gutenberg creates the printing press as a way to not only record beer recipes, but also print up directions to the party so nobody has to write it on their hands.

1620 • Pilgrims flee England for America to escape religious persecution and party as they please without the King of England calling the fuzz.

1773 • Tired of paying a cover charge to England, a bunch of Boston bros protested by throwing a Party in the Harbor—trashing the place and not cleaning up.

1820 • The Industrial Revolution takes place in America. Beer becomes mass-produced, and Party Animals begin to spread across the young country.

1920 • Prohibition strikes and makes alcohol illegal. The Party Animal does what he does best: hides from the cops and keeps partying.

1933 • Prohibition is repealed, and the Party Animal returns with force!

1953 • America's affluent youth gains strength and flexes its beer muscles. Beer Pong—staple game of the Party Animal—is invented in its earliest form at Dartmouth College.

1976 • America celebrates its 200th birthday with a nationwide party. Amazingly, almost 75 percent of the country makes it through the party without puking.

1987 • Spuds MacKenzie is born. The term Party Animal takes on a literal meaning.

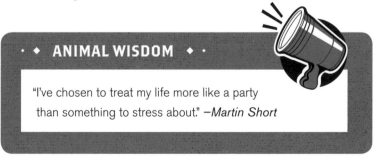

• ◆ ANIMAL WISDOM ◆ •

"I've chosen to treat my life more like a party than something to stress about." *—Martin Short*

1999 • Fearing a millennial apocalypse, Party Animals party so hard that they avoid this extinction-level event, but serious damage has been done to the kingdom's structure.

2004 • Facebook is founded. Party Animals begin spending more time online and out of the party scene.

Present • Finally recuperating from the 1999 hangover and tired of fake virtual connections, Party Animals are looking to make physical connection again and return to partying in preparation for 2999.

Party Animal Legends

TO BECOME A PARTY ANIMAL, one must stand on the shoulders of Party Animal giants. While these shoulders might not always provide the most stable support, they do provide critical perspective. A comprehensive list of all infamous partiers would be highly informative, insightful, and too close to education for the authors to condone. So what follows is a brief, subjective survey of notable Party Animals throughout history.

HISTORICAL PARTY ANIMALS

CALIGULA (Roman Emperor, Sexual Sportsman) The Charlie Sheen of his day, Caligula spent his money recklessly, slept with other men's wives for sport, killed out of boredom, organized massive orgies, and even declared himself a god. His name alone could out-party most mortals.

CASANOVA (World-Class Lover, Blackballed from Much of Europe) The world's original bad boy, Giacomo Girolamo Casanova was more than just a legendary seducer. He was also a soldier, a spy, a violinist, a magician, a librarian, and a Lothario whose hard partying got him banned from a number of European countries.

CATHERINE THE GREAT (Russian Empress, OG Freak) Catherine the Great was a hard-drinking, dirty-dancing seductress who advocated having sex six times a day and kept a rotation of 21 official lovers on hand to perform the duty. Legend has it that Catherine outsourced some of these duties to some literal stallions.

CLEOPATRA (Egyptian Queen, Sexual Tyrannosaurus) According to lore, the Queen of the Nile created a temple where she kept dozens of young lovers and claimed she could handle 100 men in a single night. Poor guys—must have been like throwing a hot dog down a pyramid hallway.

DIONYSUS (Greco-Roman Deity, Patron Party God) This mythical wine god literally invented the party (a.k.a. the bacchanalia). These weekly wild and mystic drinking festivals in honor of Dionysus were so out of control that the Senate had to inscribe a decree declaring that the partying happened only on special occasions.

MUSICIANS

LIAM AND NOEL GALLAGHER (Rock 'n' Roll Siblings, Drunken Arch-Enemies) Every party needs a wild man who's always ready to rumble, and for the past three decades that man has been both Liam and Noel Gallagher. The Gallagher Brothers are arguably better known for their brawling/drinking/drug habits and public wars than for their work in rock band Oasis, which, thankfully, has a hard time staying together.

MICK JAGGER AND KEITH RICHARDS (Rolling Stones Founders, Glimmer Twins) Scientists have provided us with answers to some of the world's most mystifying issues, but nobody can explain how Mick Jagger and Keith Richards are still alive. After all, Jagger has recklessly slept with every second person on the planet, while Richards singlehandedly kept Columbia's economy afloat for much of the '70s and '80s.

MÖTELY CRUE (The Crue, What Tommy Lee Was Less Famously In) Don't let the Aqua Net® and lipstick fool you. These '80s rockers partied on a different level. Bassist Nikki Sixx even died briefly in 1987. But somehow they are still alive and making ~~great~~ music today.

OZZY OSBOURNE (Heavy Metal Royalty, Bat-Eater) Ozzy Osbourne wasn't always a doddering old Brit. Long before slipping into senility, the "Prince of Darkness" was a first-rate hell-raiser who once bit the head off a bat, snorted a line of ants, and allegedly asked for directions to the bar upon checking into the Betty Ford Clinic.

RICK JAMES (Musician, Super Freak) When Rick James passed away in 2004, no one cried harder or longer than his drug dealer. That's because this "Super Freak" was a balls-to-the-wall partier who reportedly spent nearly $2 million on blow during his "adult" years.

ATHLETES

ANDRE THE GIANT (Professional Wrestler, the Face of OBEY) According to journalist Richard English, the 6'11" André René Rousimoff would drink over 7,000 calories a day in booze and beer alone. An infamous legend has it that he and Dusty Rhodes were too blitzed to walk from the bar to the hotel in NYC. So they "commandeered" two horse-drawn carriages—literally throwing the drivers out—and galloped home themselves.

BABE RUTH (Baseball Legend, Human Garbage Disposal) The Sultan of Swat was a champion eater and drinker who frequently went to bat with mustard smeared on his uniform. Ruth's tendency to consume anything within arm's reach even led to his hospitalization in 1925 when the brawny Baltimore native ate a dozen hot dogs and drank eight bottles of soda between games of a doubleheader.

CANADIAN WOMEN'S HOCKEY TEAM (Olympic Champs, Team-Oriented Partiers) Canada's women's hockey team took postgame celebrations to a whole new level in 2010 when they openly drank and smoked on the ice following their gold-medal victory against the U.S. That kind of commitment to partying isn't just good, it's golden.

DENNIS RODMAN (NBA Star, Cross-Dresser) This NBA Legend is one of the most notorious party animals in sports (and looks like a party too). A regular at the hottest clubs in LA and Vegas, Rodman is known/expected to get on stage to dance with go-go girls while making it rain dollar bills. The man is so dedicated to partying that for his 50th birthday, he spent *two months* celebrating.

GEORGIE BEST (~~Soccer~~ Football Star, Party-minded Financial Planner) One of Britain's most infamous playboys, this womanizing footballer was famous for saying, "I spent a lot of money on booze, birds, and fast cars—the rest I just squandered." Well played, Georgie, well played.

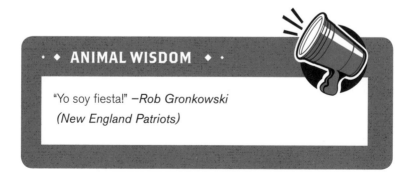

✦ ANIMAL WISDOM ✦

"Yo soy fiesta!" *—Rob Gronkowski*
(New England Patriots)

JOHN DALY **(PGA Champion, Hooters Aficionado)** You're not a true Party Animal until you've had a drink or an STD named in your honor. John Daly accomplished the former in 2010 when bars around the nation began peddling a vodka-infused lemonade named after the portly PGA champion who was once hauled off by police after passing out at a Hooters® where, it should be noted, he had the largest breasts in the establishment.

CELEBRITIES

BILL MURRAY **(Actor/Comedian, Karaoke Machine)** Known to randomly appear like a ghost of parties past, f*ckin' Bill Murray has earned a reputation as one of the world's premier party crashers. What makes it most interesting is his party preference: Instead of ritzy affairs, Murray prefers partying with the everyman, often crashing house parties and crooning with strangers at karaoke bars. He even launched his own Party Crashing Tour.

CHARLIE MURPHY **(Actor/Comedian, World-Class "+1")** It isn't easy keeping up with the likes of Prince and Rick James, but Charlie Murphy matched them blow-for-blow during the 1980s while providing security for his younger brother. And while Eddie may be the more famous of the two, Charlie is the kind of crazy-ass storyteller who will keep you entertained until you're sobering up in the morning.

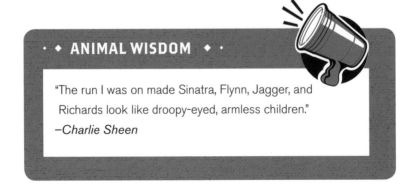

· ◆ ANIMAL WISDOM ◆ ·

"The run I was on made Sinatra, Flynn, Jagger, and Richards look like droopy-eyed, armless children."
–Charlie Sheen

CHARLIE SHEEN (Actor, Bitchin' Rock Star from Mars) Believe it or not, self-proclaimed warlock Charlie Sheen was once known more for acting than for his heroic intake of booze, drugs, and porn stars. By all accounts he should be dead by now, but like a true Party Animal, he lives on to drink another day.

DENNIS HOPPER (The Original Easy Rider, Sexual Exhibitionist) Hopper let his freak flag fly. In addition to legendary benders, he would host infamous orgies. The guest list? How about more than fifty girls. And Hopper allegedly recorded it all on tape. Makes Paris Hilton seem downright prudish.

ERROL FLYNN (Swashbuckler, Pants Unbuckler) This Hollywood legend threw infamously wild parties. His ability to mate with anything that walked is the genesis of the term "in like Flynn." Outside of the bedroom, he brandished a weapon in the Spanish Civil War and once even enjoyed a drinking bout with Fidel Castro.

HUGH HEFNER (*Playboy* Founder, Best Host in the World) For the past fifty years, no man has thrown better parties than Hugh Hefner. The founder of *Playboy* magazine, this dirty old octogenarian has transformed his sprawling Los Angeles estate into a real-life pleasure palace where celebrities, authors, astronauts, and politicians regularly come to frolic with silicone-enhanced blondes.

JACKIE GLEASON (Comedian, Drunken Mooch) A true American rags-to-riches story, Jackie Gleason grew up in the roaring '20s, but kept the roaring going for decades after. A world-class mooch, Gleason didn't let occasional debt get in the way of his partying—he often borrowed cash off buddies to keep the drinks flowing and even bribed bandleaders to play the same song all night long to drive fellow partiers nuts . . . and away from his booze.

JUDY GARLAND (Hollywood Royalty, Wicked Witch of the Rager) *The Wizard of Oz* star was a tornado of a partier. Small in size but big in destruction, she was so infamous for trashing hotel rooms that she was banned from many—causing her handlers to personally sign contracts to guarantee she would not rage. But she always did.

LINDSEY LOHAN (Actress, Career Probationer) Perhaps one of the most current examples of a true Party Girl, Lohan's debauchery was so crazy it led her to making *Herbie: Fully Loaded.* No stranger to all-night benders and drunken catfights, Lohan is a fixture at many of LA and NYC's hottest parties, so much so that she's made a new career out of appearing in tabloids for her antics—and her missing underwear.

MAE WEST (Legendary Actress, Legend on the Mattress) When God created woman he had Mae West in mind. Blonde and sultry, the curvaceous screen queen helped jumpstart the sexual revolution during the '30s and '40s with her frank attitude toward sex, which makes sense considering she once claimed to have had sex for fifteen consecutive hours. *Fifteen hours.* Some people can't even stay awake that long.

PARIS HILTON (… Um, what does she do again?) There are a lot of things that Paris Hilton is not: actress, singer, role model. What she is, however, is a true party professional who can turn a three-year-old's birthday into the hottest event in town. That's why this vacuous blonde is routinely paid hundreds of thousands of dollars to make brief appearances at restaurant openings, film premieres, birthdays, and bar mitzvahs.

ARTISTS AND WRITERS

CHARLES BUKOWSKI (Author, Dirty Old Man) Charles Bukowski, crowned by *Time* magazine as "The Laureate of American Lowlife," may not have been the best writer in the world, but he made his mark. The same could be said for his party habits: Bukowski loved boozing and chasing women, but he was terrible at it, often drinking till he puked and then going home with anything with a pulse.

ERNEST HEMINGWAY (Author, Hard-drinking Tough Guy) Few famous names are as synonymous with drunken rabblerousing as Hemingway's. Often wanting to explore the depths of manliness, Hemingway would sometimes go shark fishing and bare-knuckle boxing for fun, usually while drunk.

HUNTER S. THOMPSON (Author/Journalist, Rum Enthusiast) Thompson essentially made a career out of chronicling his drunken, drug-ridden antics. While most Party Animals know how to make an entrance, Thompson knew how to make an exit—after his suicide in 2005, he was cremated, loaded into a giant bullet, and shot out of a cannon, as requested in his will.

JACK KEROUAC (Author, Road Trip Pioneer) It's one thing to party hard for a single night, but Jack Kerouac partied nonstop for an entire year as he and his buddy Neal Cassady went on a series of booze-soaked and drug-fueled road trips across the United States. Kerouac later turned their experiences into a novel, *On The Road,* thereby giving millions of aimless college kids their own blueprint for wasting their twenties.

LORD BYRON (Poet, Rock Star of the Romantic Era) While Lord Byron may be known for his writings, he's arguably better known for being what many consider the first celebrity of Western Civilization. Byron not only achieved rock star status from his writing, but also from his hard drinkin', fast-lovin' lifestyle. Nothing the man did was small, including pet ownership: When in college, Byron was known to roll with his own tamed bear.

The Partying President, George W. Bush

We'll be the first to admit that our forty-third president was a total party pooper by the time he reached the Oval Office, but it wasn't always that way. Dubya was once a huge partier in his twenties and thirties and even drove home with a garbage can wedged under his car after an all-night bender. His penchant for booze and assigning colorful nicknames would have made this former frat boy a blast to hang out with during his prime.

OSCAR WILDE (Author, Civilized Debaucher)
During the latter part of the nineteenth century, no London soiree was complete without a visit from Oscar Wilde. The "Prince of Paradox" was a brilliant conversationalist who understood the value of idle chatter and innuendo. As he once observed, "Hear no evil, speak no evil—and you'll never be invited to a party."

FICTIONAL PARTY ANIMALS

ALAN GARNER (Zach Galifianakis: *The Hangover*)
One quarter of the legendary Wolf Pack, Alan Garner is a lovable manchild whose liberal use of Rohypnol leads to two of the most memorable bachelor parties ever captured on film. Oh, and for the record, it's not a purse, it's called a satchel. Indiana Jones wears one.

ANIMAL (*The Muppet Movie*) Animal is the primitive, crazed drummer of Dr. Teeth and The Electric Mayhem. During performances, Animal is usually chained to the drum set, as his musical outbursts are extremely violent. Many consider him to be modeled after the real-life Party Animal Keith Moon.

FRANK "THE TANK" RICARD (Will Ferrell: _Old School_) Frank Ricard may appear a buttoned-down suburbanite, but percolating just beneath the surface is a wild man who's two beers away from streaking through the quad. His loyalty to his friends and brazen commitment to public nudity make him a must for any social gathering.

JEFF SPICOLI (Sean Penn: _Fast Times at Ridgemont High_) A stoner since the third grade, Jeff Spicoli is a longhaired SoCal surf bum who understands that all you really need in life are "some tasty waves and a cool buzz." His unflappable ability to live in the moment makes him one of the most bitchin' partiers in cinematic history.

JOHN "BLUTO" BLUTARSKY (John Belushi: _Animal House_) The true heart and soul of the Deltas, Bluto is a hard-drinking, class-cutting slob who boldly ignores his homework and tutorials in favor of toga parties and food fights. Sure, he may not know who bombed Pearl Harbor, but his desire to let loose at all costs is beyond reproach.

THEODORE LOGAN AND BILL S. PRESTON, ESQUIRE (Keanu Reeves and Alex Winter: _Bill & Ted's Excellent Adventure_) Nearly anyone can party with their peers, but it takes a special breed of Party Animal to trip the light fantastic with Billy the Kid, Socrates, Joan of Arc, Genghis Khan, and Abraham Lincoln. Bill and Ted partied that hard and _still_ managed to get their final turned in on time.

VAN WILDER (Ryan Reynolds: _Van Wilder_) The coolest cat at Coolidge College, Van Wilder is a golf-cart-riding, dean-needling professional party liaison who has enjoyed more than a few of the school's student bodies. Voluntarily in school for seven years, this perpetual undergrad understands the true value of staying in school.

The Metamorphosis of a Party Animal

A Party Animal does not magically hatch fully-formed and ready to rock.
They develop like Homo Sapiens through several life stages as shown below.

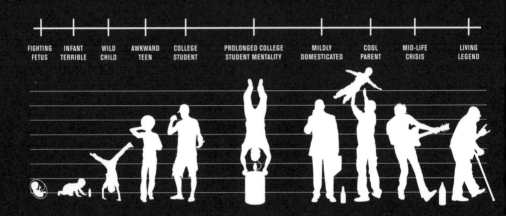

FIGHTING FETUS | INFANT TERRIBLE | WILD CHILD | AWKWARD TEEN | COLLEGE STUDENT | PROLONGED COLLEGE STUDENT MENTALITY | MILDLY DOMESTICATED | COOL PARENT | MID-LIFE CRISIS | LIVING LEGEND

Awesome Party Animal Occupations

Some careers are swimming with Party Animals. Here are some
common farm teams for future lives of the parties.

MUSICIAN

BARTENDER

PRO ATHLETE

ARTIST

CELEBRITY

COMEDIAN

CLUB PROMOTER

**STAY-AT-HOME SON
OR DAUGHTER**

**EDDIE MURPHY'S
GIRL IN 1985**

Common Types of Party Animals

AS WE'VE SEEN, the Party Animal is a distinct organism. But don't assume the Party Animal is a homogenous category. Like Darwin's finches (what up, finches?), the Party Animal has evolved into many subspecies—each perfectly evolved for a different area of the social ecosystem. The differentiation allows the subspecies to populate the same party environment but avoid overt competition for resources.

The following taxonomy is based on the most accurate scientific conjecture available and should be used as a guide to help understand the thick and dense jungle that is the Party Animal Kingdom.

• ◆ PARTY FACT ◆ •

"Hair of the Dog" is a metaphor for a hangover treatment that dates back to A.D. 79. Originally a recipe for inserting a biting dog's tail hair into the bite wound to prevent rabies and other evil consequences, Hair of the Dog now refers to consuming more alcohol to lessen the effects of a hangover.

The Wolf
LUPUS PARTIUS

Rally Cry
(permanent scream)

No Watch
(always happy hour)

Whiskey
(no glassware required)

T-Shirt and Jeans
(rarely washed)

Chuck Taylors
(famous drinking shoes)

In the Party Animal Kingdom the wolf is king—sorry lions. These Alpha males and females are social animals by nature and constantly search for epic ragers. The wolf is unrivaled in its ability to track down and dominate any type of party.

Defining Characteristic	Although some wolves roam alone, most travel in a pack, or entourage, so to speak. In other words, they bring their party with them.
Common Features	Intense eyes, constant snarl, striking pose.
Unique Fact	The Wolf's howl—or rallying cry—is the universal signal to party. Party Animals of all types react and travel great distances to join the party when they hear the cry.

The Raccoon

LOTOR PARTIUS

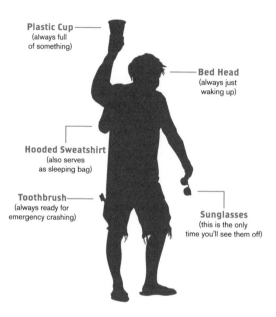

Plastic Cup
(always full
of something)

Bed Head
(always just
waking up)

Hooded Sweatshirt
(also serves
as sleeping bag)

Toothbrush
(always ready for
emergency crashing)

Sunglasses
(this is the only
time you'll see them off)

These unsuspecting creatures are an anomaly to say the least. By day, they are as average and calm as can be, often unnoticed by other Party Animals. But once the sun goes down, their party craving goes up. They move with effortless grace through the night—only knocking over trash cans on purpose.

Defining Characteristic	Nocturnal partier—the later it gets, the harder they rock.
Common Features	Heightened senses, omnipresent sunglasses, permanent bedhead.
Unique Fact	The Raccoon has no comprehension of the daytime world—he would be amazed that people wake up before noon.

The Fox

VULPES PARTIUS

Spirit Hands
(declares her position)

Mixed Drink
(any kind of _____tini)

Intoxicating Scent
(even smells hot)

No Purse
(never gets ID'd and
drinks are always free)

Designer Heels
(for breaking hearts
and free admittance)

This species oozes sensuality. She is the epitome of the female Party Animal. She can party as hard as anyone and looks and smells better than everyone while doing it. Other females want to be her and males want to be with her.

Defining Characteristic	Mischievous and cunning, she always gets what she wants. She can outfox the common partier.
Common Features	Attractive, perfectly peacocked (see page 116), always in makeup.
Unique Fact	As the female Fox ages, she becomes a Cougar. Her prey, however, stay the same age.

The Hawk

AVES PARTIUS

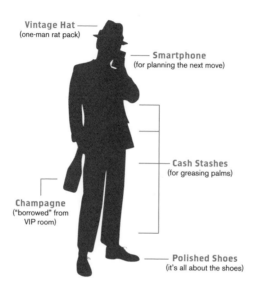

Vintage Hat (one-man rat pack)

Smartphone (for planning the next move)

Cash Stashes (for greasing palms)

Champagne ("borrowed" from VIP room)

Polished Shoes (it's all about the shoes)

When someone asks, "Who is the brains of this operation?" everyone points to this Party Animal. These geniuses have applied themselves to the quest for the eternal buzz—instead of the quest for a cure to athlete's foot. These pros are all business—and never look back.

Defining Characteristic	Mastering the master plan for the night.
Common Features	Always above the fray, looking to swoop down to take advantage of an opportunity.
Unique Fact	Considered "lucky" by outsiders, the Hawk makes his luck—and his own fake IDs.

The Tiger

TIGRIS PARTIUS

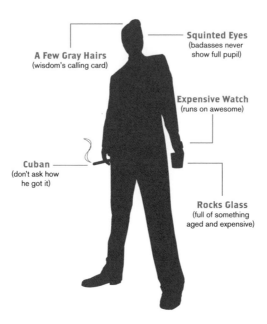

A Few Gray Hairs
(wisdom's calling card)

Squinted Eyes
(badasses never
show full pupil)

Expensive Watch
(runs on awesome)

Cuban
(don't ask how
he got it)

Rocks Glass
(full of something
aged and expensive)

A commanding figure, the Tiger is often considered the most interesting partier in the world. They are the life of most parties, even if they're not there. They have tangoed with legends and have lived to tell the tales. Just being in the same room as the Tiger can turn you into a Party Animal through osmosis.

Defining Characteristic	Unfazed. Completely. Utterly. Unfazed.
Common Features	Cool, calm, and collected. The Tiger has only one emotion—awesome.
Unique Fact	Discerning. A Tiger shows good judgment in all aspects of partying: from drinking to dressing to dropping names. Always under control, always making the right move.

The Weasel

MUSTELA PARTIUS

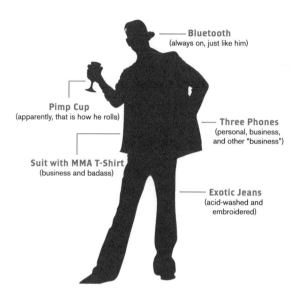

Bluetooth
(always on, just like him)

Pimp Cup
(apparently, that is how he rolls)

Three Phones
(personal, business,
and other "business")

Suit with MMA T-Shirt
(business and badass)

Exotic Jeans
(acid-washed and
embroidered)

If the Fox oozes sensuality, the Weasel oozes cheese. Velveeta®, to be exact. This smooth talker can charm his way into the club—or your pants. The Weasel is much better to go to a party with—rather than meet at a party.

Defining Characteristic	The Gift of Gab. Flattery gets them everywhere.
Common Features	Great teeth, impeccably dressed, owns multiple cell phones.
Unique Fact	Yes, in fact, they actually do start believing their own bullshit.

The Iguana

LACERTILLIA PARTIUS

Big Hat
(keeps sun out of
eyes and bald spot)

No Shirt
(no problem)

Perma Tan
(SPF WTF?)

Margarita
(in a bottomless
plastic cup)

Jean Shorts
(made 'em himself)

This Party Animal's quest for the eternal buzz continues today—and every day. He absorbs energy from the sun. But does as little as possible to expend any. Some call him beach bum. Others just call him dude.

Defining Characteristic	Chill to the point of sloth.
Common Features	Perma tan, flip-flops or barefoot, doesn't own a tie.
Unique Fact	The Iguana never got around to getting a driver's license. And doesn't see anything weird about that.

The Puppy

CANINUS PARTIUS

Backward Cap
(gotta sw-sw-switch it up!)

Energy Drink
(gotta keep it up!)

Ironic T-Shirt
(gotta start the convo!)

YOLO Tattoo
(gotta live every day!)

High Tops
(gotta move quick!)

Hyper excitable with a short attention sp... oh look, a squirrel! Where were we? They are up for anything, not because they have been there and bonged that, but because they have the unstoppable energy of youth on their side. And their parents still pay for almost everything. Of all the animals, Puppies are most often sober Party Animals—just getting high on life.

Defining Characteristic | Unbounded energy and naiveté.
Common Features | YOLO tattoo, YOLO shirt, fine whiskers over the upper lip.
Unique Fact | The Puppy keeps his social media ecosystem fully populated with every detail of his life. Oh look, he just tweeted that he read this sentence.

Other Party Animal Species

THE PARTY ANIMAL KINGDOM has a panoply of other notable creatures. Here is just a sampler platter of them.

FLOUNDER

The permanent bro who is eternally fratastic and bleeds his school colors—even if he's balding in the suburbs.

PENGUIN

The unsuspecting Penguin appears awkward but comes into his own—and comes out—at black tie events.

SHARK

This animal works hard and parties even harder. Once business hours end, the Shark feeds on parties rather than PowerPoints.

ANTELOPE

These young, bouncy, female Party Animals move in a synchronized yet often oblivious herd.

SNAKE

The creepy "porn" guy who slithers around at the end of the party looking for a wounded Antelope to attack.

TASMANIAN DEVIL

This is a train wreck live and in the flesh, who barrels through the party like a hurricane.

Mystical Party Animals

CENTAUR ◆

Half man, half horse, the Centaur is thought to be the first metamorphasis of a human into a Party Animal–a very well-endowed Party Animal.

UNICORN ◆

Believed to be the most pure of all Party Animals,
the Unicorn is now a symbol of chivalry amongst fellow partiers.

PHOENIX ◆

This immortal Party Animal is said to rise from the ashes every 500 years to rage like none other. The last known sighting was in 1704.

MERMAID ◆

This benevolent creature was known to spread love and cheers throughout the beach party scenes in ancient Assyria.

DRAGON ◆

The most notorious of all Party Animals, the Dragon dominated the party scenes throughout China and Europe, leaving a path of destruction and party fouls in its wake.

GRIFFIN ◆

An especially powerful and majestic Party Animal, the Griffin is thought to be the pre-mortal king of all the animals–half eagle, half lion, all party.

Party Parasites

THERE ARE SOME WANNA-BE PARTIERS that claim to be a part of the Party Animal Kingdom but actually just exploit and harm the entire species. Know them and avoid them at all costs.

PARTY POOPER

They show up to a party but never have any fun. Often seen alone in a corner texting, they never participate in any social activities and try to get everyone to leave early.

GAME KILLER

Sometimes referred to as a Crotch Block, these anti-wingmen have the ability to interfere with a Party Animal's ability to hook up with a potential mate, often going to extreme measures to prevent deals from being sealed.

ONE-UPPER

Anything you can do, they can do better. The One-Upper seems like a Party Animal, but they show their exaggerated colors when they just happen to always have a story that always tops yours.

THE PLANNER

This parasite simply makes plans to party and will continue to plan out every aspect of the night. They are even known to try and issue an itinerary of activities. Party Animals do not follow plans, they laugh at them.

THE OLD MAN

He's shaking his cane at you and begging for you to get off his yard for a reason—he's older than fun itself.

Party Animal VS Asshole VS Alcoholic

Party Animal	Asshole	Alcoholic
• Has fun with others	• Has fun at others' expense	• Has fun at own expense
• Down for whatever	• Down to complain	• Down to pass out
• Has an entourage	• Has an accomplice	• Has a sponsor
• Gets laid	• Gets beat-up	• Gets DUI
• Involved in shenanigans	• Involved in bullying	• Involved in blackouts

• ◆ ANIMAL WISDOM ◆ •

"I definitely want to be remembered as a person who believes in family. And it would also be nice to be remembered as a Party Animal!" *–Kat Von D*

Fueling the Beast

◆

PROPER DIET
AND HYDRATION

◆

PARTY ANIMALS FUEL THE PARTY. But what fuels the Party Animal? Certainly her insatiable love of life and desire to lead a life worth living are critical. But a Party Animal cannot live on cliché motivational posters alone.

No, a Party Animal's diet is critical to her ability to survive, thrive, and stage dive. It must fuel the activity, satisfy the primal craving, and help cultivate a killer buzz.

So this chapter will cover the actual eating and drinking habits of the Party Animal. It will look at the most important chemicals, substances, and post-party foodstuffs that fuels the Party Animal.

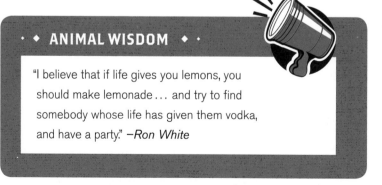

· ◆ **ANIMAL WISDOM** ◆ ·

"I believe that if life gives you lemons, you should make lemonade . . . and try to find somebody whose life has given them vodka, and have a party." –*Ron White*

PARTY ANIMALS HAVE FINE CONTROL over their behavior. Part of that control is knowing how to alter it—mainly through mind-altering chemicals. No, not those serious banned substances that can mess you up for life. Ok, maybe those substances, but we're not covering that here. This section catalogs the most common sources of a buzz, the state of chemical-induced euphoria that many—but not all—Party Animals chase.

CAFFEINE
WHAT IS IT?

$$CH_3$$
$$O$$
$$N \quad N$$
$$N \quad N$$
$$CH_3$$
$$H_3C$$
$$O$$

Caffeine is a bitter white alkaloid found in varying quantities in the seeds, leaves, and fruit of some plants, where it acts as a natural pesticide that paralyzes and kills certain insects. But it also powers Party Animals through the night and helps them in the mornings.

WHAT DOES IT DO?

It is the world's most widely consumed psychoactive drug. For one big reason: It's legal, unregulated, and awesome. Ok, that was three.

PROS: This stimulant shoots right through the central nervous system. It increases attention, decreases fatigue, and has even been shown to lower the risk of cardiovascular disease and some cancers.

CONS: It can increase blood pressure, reduce fine motor control, and make you pee—a lot.

HOW DO WE GET IT? Globally, we chug an estimated 120,000 tons of caffeine a year—which equals one serving of a caffeinated beverage for every person every day. So get sipping.

Chocolate • This contains a small dose of caffeine and often a minimal effect.

Tea • Tea is consumed more than coffee and contains more caffeine by dry weight. But it provides less of a buzz since it's brewed weaker.

Soft Drinks • It's a common ingredient in soft drinks, especially cola, which is originally prepared from Kola nuts.

Coffee • The world's second most traded commodity packs a serious buzz for Party Animals everywhere.

Energy Drinks • Additional caffeine that has been taken out of decaffeinated coffee beans is often added back into these soft drinks on steroids.

Pills • Several forms of caffeine pills exist for all-nighters—of the study and the party varieties.

CAFFEINE CURES

While it's been scientifically proven that caffeine doesn't actually sober you up, that doesn't mean that it doesn't belong on the Party Animal utility belt. It has been proven to help people think and feel like they're more sober, and remember, *feeling* sober is half the battle!

SOBER SHOT Take a spoonful of ground coffee, place on tongue. With tongue, push against roof of mouth and begin sucking on the grinds, essentially making your own coffee with your spit. This potent, concentrated shot of caffeine will shock your system enough to clear your head for a short time as well as cover any alcohol on the breath. Great for when you need to talk to the cops who busted up the party.

HANGOVER CURE Mixing caffeine with aspirin will help alleviate the hangover symptoms that often follow a night of partying. While it helps handle the headaches and pains on the morning after, it still won't help explain why you thought it was a good idea to steal your neighbor's mailbox.

SODA CHUG While not ideal, soda consumption is believed by many to help make a hangover more bearable, thanks to its eye-widening caffeine, its rehydrating fluids, and the sugars that can be used to replace some of what you lost the night before. There's no medical proof supporting it, but plenty of Party Animals swear by it.

Stages of the Caffeine Buzz

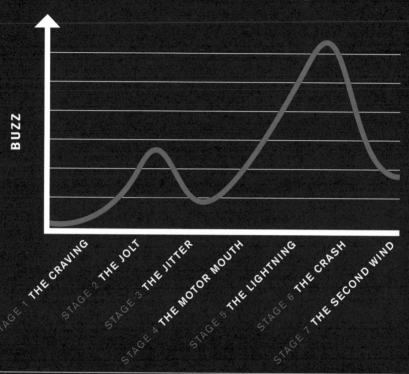

BUZZ

STAGE 1 THE CRAVING

STAGE 2 THE JOLT

STAGE 3 THE JITTER

STAGE 4 THE MOTOR MOUTH

STAGE 5 THE LIGHTNING

STAGE 6 THE CRASH

STAGE 7 THE SECOND WIND

The Power of the Party Nap

Sleep is overrated—and a true Party Animal knows slumber is no place to rock out. So science comes to the rescue. The solution is a caffeine-powered party nap. It has four steps:

1. Drink a cup of coffee.
2. Set alarm for 15 minutes.
3. Immediately lie down for power nap.
4. Do backflip thing out of the bed.

It takes caffeine about 15 minutes to start having a noticeable effect on the body—at least, enough to keep you awake. Theoretically, the party nap should allow the coffee to kick in right as you're waking up from the nap. Boom, there you go.

NICOTINE

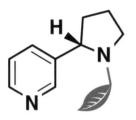

Like caffeine, this is another naturally occurring liquid alkaloid. It comes from the leaves of the *Solanaceae* family of plants, which includes petunias, tomatoes, potatoes, deadly nightshade, and the most infamous of all, tobacco. Nicotine is named after the tobacco plant *Nicotiana tabacum*, which in turn is named after the French ambassador to Portugal, Jean Nicot de Villemain, who sent tobacco and seeds to Paris in 1560 and promoted its medicinal use.

WHAT DOES IT DO?

It's a registered pesticide, but in low doses it acts as a simulant in mammals. (Psst, that includes you.) Nicotine diffuses quickly into the bloodstream through skin, lungs, and mucous membranes—like those in the nose and mouth.

PROS: Many Party Animals enjoy the "biphasic" effects—it can both relax and energize the animal. Some attribute it to improving concentration and alertness.

CONS: It's highly addictive—even more habit-forming than cocaine, according to some researchers. It increases blood pressure and the risk of heart disease. And many products that contain nicotine have their own risks of bad stuff like cancer, emphysema, strokes, and burning down your house.

HOW DO WE GET IT? Here are the most common ways a Party Animal consumes are nicotine.

·· BUZZ ··

Cigars • The indigenous people of the Caribbean puffed on these rolls of tobacco leaves long before Columbus' crew introduced them to generations of rich white guys.

·· BUZZ ··

Bidis/Beedis • These thin, flavored sticks are like cigarettes but wrapped in a leaf from the Asian tendu plant.

·· BUZZ ··

Cigarettes • The offspring of cigars, these tobacco-filled paper cylinders are public enemy number one—and tobacco product number one as well.

·· BUZZ ··

Electronic cigarettes • These devices use a small heating element to create a nicotine mist that is inhaled by those looking to stop smoking or be on a reality TV show.

·· BUZZ ··

Pipe • While pipes date back to the Romans and Greeks for smoking hashish, it was later that New World peoples who first started putting tobacco in there instead.

·· BUZZ ··

Dip / Chew / Snus • Terms American Party Animals use for a finely chopped, smokeless tobacco that is placed in the mouth and packs a serious nicotine punch.

Stages of the Cigarette Buzz

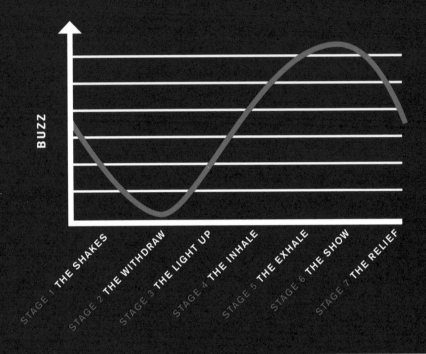

BUZZ

STAGE 1 THE SHAKES

STAGE 2 THE WITHDRAW

STAGE 3 THE LIGHT UP

STAGE 4 THE INHALE

STAGE 5 THE EXHALE

STAGE 6 THE SHOW

STAGE 7 THE RELIEF

Cigarette Slang:

BOGIES

BUTT

CIG

CANCER STICK

FRAJO

GRIT

LUNG CANDY

NAIL

NIC STICK

SMOKE

SMOKY TREAT

SQUARE

VITAMIN N

THC (DELTA-9-TETRAHYDROCANNABINOL)

THC is the leader of the cannabinoids, a gang of psychoactive chemicals found in the leaves and buds of the *Cannabis sativa* and *Cannabis indica* plants. The plants are indigenous to Central and South Asia, but there have been reports of a nearly 3,000-year-old Egyptian mummy containing traces of THC. It's now grown and consumed around the world. And although banned by the U.S. federal government in 1937, it is estimated that 45 million Americans regularly use marijuana, which is roughly the population of Spain.

WHAT DOES IT DO?

THC is a very potent psychoactive chemical that enters the bloodstream very quickly. While the initial effects will wear off after an hour or two, the chemicals remain in your system much longer.

PROS: The primary reason for consumption is that it makes you high as a kite. But according to Clint Werner, author of *Marijuana: Gateway to Health,* it also has been proven that THC helps the brain recover from the effects of binge drinking by regenerating new brain cells (replacing those that alcohol kills off). THC also helps those who have suffered from glaucoma, concussions, and other head injuries.

CONS: Additionally, marijuana affects motor coordination, increases your heart rate, and, for some, raises levels of anxiety. Studies also show that marijuana smoke contains traces of cancer-causing chemicals similar to those associated with cigarettes.

HOW DO WE GET IT? Cannabis has been consumed the same ways for tens of thousands of years—by smoking it or eating it.

·· BUZZ ··

SMOKABLE FORMS Light it up and smoke it. Here are the many ways to combust the weed:

Pipe • Available in metal, glass, ceramic, or homemade from apples or discarded beer cans.

Bong or Hookah • A weapon of mass consumption with a water chamber to filter the smoke.

Joints • Weed rolled in smoking papers.

Blunts • The joint's bigger brother, rolled in a tobacco leaf or cigar wrapper.

Vaporizers • A fancy contraption that vaporizes the THC and is said to be more efficient and "healthier" than smoking.

THE BOOK OF THE PARTY ANIMAL

·· BUZZ ··

EDIBLE FORMS These include cookies, brownies, and other food products. Because of the way the body processes the THC, edibles deliver a more potent experience than smoked forms.

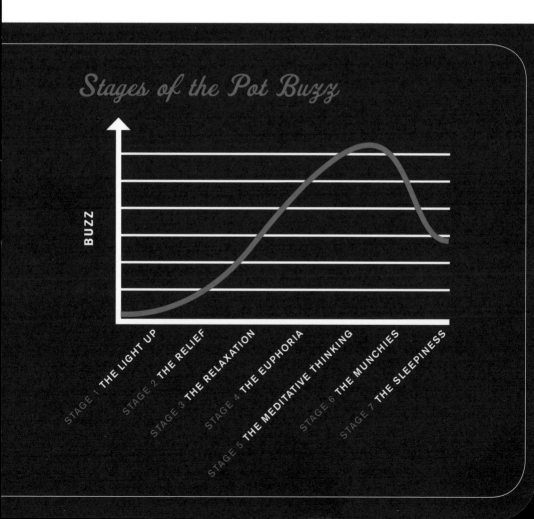

Stages of the Pot Buzz

BUZZ

STAGE 1 THE LIGHT UP

STAGE 2 THE RELIEF

STAGE 3 THE RELAXATION

STAGE 4 THE EUPHORIA

STAGE 5 THE MEDITATIVE THINKING

STAGE 6 THE MUNCHIES

STAGE 7 THE SLEEPINESS

THE MOUTH-TO-NOSE A staple of smokers. Simply take a drag, inhale, then breathe out with just your nose, letting the smoke escape from there. This tried-and-true trick shows off the vast duct system that is human respiration.

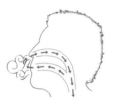

FRENCH INHALE Show your cultural side with this elegant inhale. After taking a drag, open your mouth, allowing the smoke to wallow out. As it exits the mouth, begin inhaling with your nose.

STASH AND GRAB After taking a hit, blow the smoke slowly into the inside of your jacket. If done slowly enough, the smoke will sit there for a second; as it begins to escape, inhale it back in and blow it back out where you please.

HOW TO MANAGE THE MUNCHIES

One peculiar phenomenon associated with marijuana use is the increased hunger that users feel, often called the "munchies." Research shows that marijuana increases food enjoyment and the number of times a person eats each day.

The best way to deal with this is, well, to give in. Elise McDonough, author of *The Official High Times Cannabis Cookbook,* has this to say: While the stereotype exists of stoners as "junk food junkies," any true hedonist knows that food should be a sensual experience that's comforting and satisfying—so make two grilled cheese sandwiches, and put a burger in between them.

Respect the Headiquette

by Elise McDonough, *High Times*

"Headiquette" is the system of manners that governs pot sharing. Here are several finer points.

- "Puff Puff Pass" is the first commandment, followed by "Pass the Dutchie to the left hand side."

- Don't hold the joint and pontificate: Take your puffs and move it along. "Dude, it's not a microphone" is the appropriate phrase for a joint hog.

- Never get a bunch of saliva on the end of a perfectly rolled spliff.

- Be sure to allow any late arrivals to "catch up" with a few extra hits.

- Don't ask where the weed came from, how much it costs, or if you can score any! Save that for close friends only, and ask privately.

Marijuana Slang

Does weed by any other name smell as funky? You be the judge. Here are a handful of synonyms for that sticky green stuff.

ASTROTURF	GRASS	LIMBO	SKUNK
BEASTERS	GREEN	MARY JANE	SMOKE
BUD	HEADIES	MOTHER	STICKY ICKY
BUDDHA	HERB	NUGS	SWAG
CHRONIC	HYDRO	POT	TREES
DANK	INDO	REEFER	VIPE
GANJA	KAYA	SINSEMILLA	

ALCOHOL

WHAT IS IT?

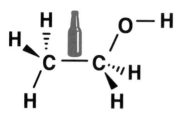

The alcohol found in alcoholic beverages is ethyl alcohol. That sounds scary so we just call it alcohol. In its pure form it's colorless, odorless, and highly flammable. But thankfully, it is very mixable and comes in many deliciously diluted forms. The intoxicating effects of ethanol consumption have been known since ancient times. A true Party Animal needs to know all of the ins and outs for this powerful liquid.

WHAT DOES IT DO?

While people can respond to alcohol differently, it is classified as a depressant as it suppresses some activities in the central nervous system. That's a buzz-kill way of describing a buzz.

PROS: While studies show some health benefits of moderate alcohol consumption (including reduced risk of heart disease), the most obvious benefits are relaxation and socialization: Both contributing factors to a happier life.

CONS: Heavy consumption has been shown to increase the risks of certain cancers and damage to the liver. Secondarily, alcohol intoxication can lead to unsafe behaviors like drunk driving.

HOW DO WE GET IT? Two words: fermentation and distillation. These two processes are what we can thank for the bevy of beverages before us.

FERMENTED BEVERAGES These drinks come from the basic conversion of sugars into alcohol by yeast.

Beer ◆ A bread soup made from cereal grains and seasoned with hops, a relative of cannabis.

Cider ◆ Often made from apples or pears, ciders are close cousins to beer.

Wine ◆ Grapes that are squashed, fermented, sometimes aged, and always enjoyed.

DISTILLED BEVERAGES These drinks known as spirits go the extra step—taking fermented liquids and further isolating the alcohol from the mixture, making them more potent.

Brandy ◆ A fancy name for distilled wine. Cognac is a fancier brandy made only in one area of France.

Gin ◆ One of the many beverages based on a neutral-grain spirit with additional flavorings, in this case, juniper berries.

Liqueur / Cordial • Alcohol that is bottled with added sugars and often flavored with fruit, cream, herbs, spices, flowers, or even nuts.

Rum • Starting with sugarcane or molasses, rum is distilled and filtered to create different variants.

Tequila • The agave is a giant relative of the lily that grows in Mexico; its sugars are fermented and turned into this infamous spirit.

Vodka • This grain spirit can use any fermented material (from grapes to grain to potatoes) thoroughly distilled to become neutral in its flavor.

Whisk(e)y / Scotch • Similar ingredients to beer, just distilled and often aged in wood barrels.

• ◆ ANIMAL WISDOM ◆ •

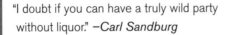

"I doubt if you can have a truly wild party without liquor." *–Carl Sandburg*

THE BOOK OF THE PARTY ANIMAL

Stages of the Alcohol Buzz

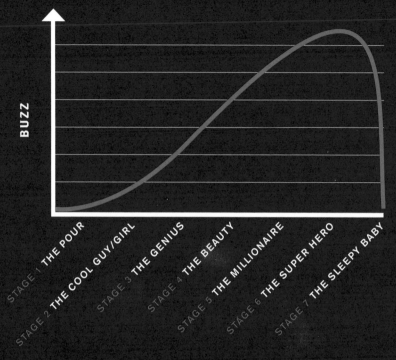

BUZZ

STAGE 1 THE POUR

STAGE 2 THE COOL GUY/GIRL

STAGE 3 THE GENIUS

STAGE 4 THE BEAUTY

STAGE 5 THE MILLIONAIRE

STAGE 6 THE SUPER HERO

STAGE 7 THE SLEEPY BABY

Booze Slang

ALCAMAHOL	COURAGE	HOOCH	POISON
ASS WHUP	DRANK	JUICE	SAUCE
BOOZE	ELIXIR	LIQUID COURAGE	SHINE
BROTH	FIREWATER		THE BOTTLE
COBRA PISS	GIGGLE WATER		TIPPLE

Another Species of Party Animal

In a study appearing in *The Journal of Addiction Biology* (a must read for a professional Party Animal), researchers tested the influence of bonding on alcohol consumption with prairie voles. The mice-like creatures were given a choice to sip from two bottles—one water and one a 6-percent alcohol solution. When alone in cages, the voles drank nearly equal amounts of plain water and alcohol-spiked water. But when housed in pairs, they partied down and drank four-fifths of their fluid intake from the alcohol-spiked source. But that isn't all: the pairs also matched each other drink for drink. Whether they trashed their cages and ordered pizza is still unclear.

How to Drink Like a Party Animal

THROW AWAY GARNISHES: That orange slice is pretty, but leave it for soccer practice. Toss it with those little umbrellas.

HAVE A USUAL: Find a home base, a bar you can call your own. Tip well and order consistently. In no time, you'll be able to say, "I'll have the usual, Sammy."

NO TINY SIPPING: This is not because we advocate chugging. Which we may or may not. It's because most drinks won't taste right with a little sip. A full-mouth mini-gulp will better rep the flavor.

DON'T LEAVE BEFORE BUYING YOUR ROUND: If the group is taking turns buying rounds, make sure you don't screw up the rotation. Don't be known as Sally Skip Out.

SHARE GENEROUSLY: Most people have no idea what they are drinking. They drink in the same rut unless someone helps them step outside their routine and expand their drink-a-verse. That's you.

THE TOP SIX PARTY ANIMAL DRINKS

1. JELL-O® SHOTS

According the book *Jelly Shot Test Kitchen*, a forefather (or mother) of these wiggling shots was created by French bakers in the early 1800s. Today, less French people also enjoy it the world over. A Party Animal never turns down a well-made Jell-O® Shot.

PRO: Everyone loves a giggly Jell-O®—and it's been proven that you can't frown and eat one at the same time.

CON: Runny ones can be the stickiest substance known to man.

TOP JELL-O® SHOT TIPS

1. **Master the Recipe** · The general rule of sticky thumb is to dissolve 3 ounces of Jell-O® in 1 cup of boiling water, then add 8 ounces of cold liquid—either full strength booze or a mixture of booze and cold water.

2. **Avoid Fresh Pineapple** · This prickly fruit contains a badass enzyme that dissolves proteins. Gelatin is made from animal proteins and it won't set up with pineapple in its presence.

3. **Sweet Release** · If you made the Jell-O® Shots in a metal pan, let it rest in another pan of warm water to help it slide out.

4. **Attempt the Jell-O® Bomb** · This is a Jell-O® Shot that's packing heat. Fill and chill half of a Bundt cake pan with your mixture. Once solid,

insert several airplane bottles around it and cover with more mixture. Chill, invert, serve, eat, and drink the bottles when done.

2. THE LONG ISLAND ICED TEA

The infamous Long Island Ice Tea has been the source of many drunken nights and many blackouts. We think. But this is to be expected with a drink that is over 90 percent liquor and does not taste like it. And while there is no iced tea is the drink, there are over 780 calories! Each ounce of liquor hovers around 100+ calories and the only other things diluting the drink are packed with sugars. Talk about Strong Island.

THE RECIPE

1 part vodka	1 part triple sec
1 part tequila	1½ parts sweet
1 part rum	and sour mix
1 part gin	1 splash Coca-Cola®

Mix ingredients together over ice in a glass. Pour into a shaker and give one brisk shake. Pour back into the glass and make sure there is a touch of fizz at the top.

· ◆ PARTY FACT ◆ ·

In Utah, bartenders cannot legally serve a proper Long Island Iced Tea due to the state's liquor laws regarding the number and amount of spirits that can go into one drink.

OTHER VARIANTS

Beverly Hills Iced Tea · Cola is replaced with champagne

Flint, Michigan Iced Tea · Cola is replaced with Vernors® Ginger Ale

Harvard Iced Tea · Cola is replaced with champagne, tequila is replaced with gin

Long Beach Iced Tea · Cola is replaced with cranberry juice

Pittsburgh Tea · Tequila is replaced with Wild Turkey

Tennessee Iced Tea · Tequila is replaced with Jack Daniel's

3. HOMEMADE HOOCH

There are few things more badass than booze that subverts the system. And nothing subverts the legal and gastrointestinal systems like bootlegged booze. True Party Animals must know their way around the seedy underbelly of alcohol—so here's a primer.

Moonshine · Moonshine is any distilled spirit made in an unlicensed still. Also known as white lightning, mountain dew, hooch, "Tennessee white whiskey," and many other names, it is a very high, often 190 proof (95 percent alcohol) distilled spirit. Many un-aged whiskeys are marketing themselves as moonshine, even though they are made in legal stills. A true Party Animal knows the real deal.

Bathtub gin · The term first appeared in 1920, in the Prohibition-era United States, in reference to a homemade spirit made under amateur conditions. As gin was the predominant drink during that time, many variations were created by mixing cheap grain alcohol with water and flavorings. Contrary to popular belief, the spirit was not always made in a bathtub. Rather, because the preferred sort of bottle was too tall to be topped off with water from a sink, they were filled from a bathtub tap.

Poteen • This is Ireland's version of moonshine. Traditionally distilled from malted barley grain or potatoes, it is one of the strongest alcoholic beverages in the world, and for centuries was illegal even in Ireland.

Pruno • This is the infamous prison wine that we hope you are lucky enough to never try in its natural setting. It is made from apples, oranges, fruit cocktail, ketchup, sugar, and possibly other ingredients, including crumbled bread. Bread supposedly provides the yeast for the pruno to ferment. The end result has been colorfully described as a vomit-flavored wine cooler.

4. GRAIN PUNCH

A.k.a. Hunch Punch, Jungle Juice, Trash Can Punch, or PGA Punch, Grain Punch is basically party in liquid form. It's simple, cheap, and completely dangerous. It often uses grain alcohol masked by fruit juice—thus walking a fine line between a good buzz and permanent blindness. It is very flexible in its ingredients and receptacles, so it's important to remember the golden ratio recipe.

THE BOOK OF THE PARTY ANIMAL

THE GOLDEN RATIO RECIPE

3 parts ice

3 parts fruit punch (or powdered mix combined with water)

2 parts ice cold grain alcohol

Mix it all together. Seriously. Just pour it all into a pitcher and begin raging.

OPTIONAL RECEPTACLES:

Fishbowl • Remove fish, rinse, fill it up with magic liquid and straws, and then drink like a fish.

Keg tub • A large plastic tub, dragged onto the deck or backyard, makes a convenient vessel for crap-loads of this stuff.

Plastic cooler • A well-cleaned plastic cooler is great for camping or tailgates. Stir with a Wiffle Ball® bat for extra flair.

Trash can • This is the most classic way to serve: Line your can with a quality trash bag first. Consider placing dry ice at the bottom of the can (before lining with the bag) to keep it cold and classy all night long.

LET YOUR FRUIT FLAG FLY

For extra tastiness, add chopped fruit like grapes, pineapple, and apples to the mixture.

For extra buzziness, soak said fruit in the alcohol overnight first.

5. CHEAP LIGHT BEER

Beer is one of the most historically significant beverages on the planet—with a rich storied past dating back to 4200 B.C. Now ignore all that and focus on washing down a fiery hot wing at a sports bar. You don't need history, you need refreshment and a buzz.

Popularized in the late 1960s, Light Beer reduces the calories by reducing the alcohol content as well as carbohydrates. The result is a pale, watery, less-flavorful swill that is awesome to pound.

TIPS FOR DRINKING CHEAP LIGHT BEER

Colder the better • The colder the temperature the less flavor to taste. Light beers are inherently bland brews, but they also can have some off-flavors that are best hidden under the cold.

Be a Pourin' star • These beers are highly carbonated—which means gas goes in so it needs to come out later. To reduce the stomach music, pour it into a wide–mouth cup and let it breath for a moment. The flatness will pay off.

Defoam finger • Dissolve excess head from a beer with your own natural oil. Simply rub a finger along a section of your face then swirl that finger through the beer and watch the foam retreat into thin air.

6. BOMBS

Often referred to as bombs or depth charges, these drinks involve dropping a shot of hard stuff into a glass of softer stuff and chugging the mix down. Not for the faint of heart—or stomach.

Boiler Maker • A shot of whiskey or bourbon dropped into a beer.
Irish Car Bomb • A mixed shot of Irish cream and Irish whiskey dropped into a pint of Irish Stout.
Sake Bomb • A shot of warm sake dropped into a cold glass of lager.
Prohibidos • A shot of blanco tequila dropped into a half-full pint of Mexican beer rimmed with salt.
Jägerbomb • A shot of Jägermeister® with Red Bull® or another energy drink. In German-speaking countries, it is called a "Turbojäger."
Skittle Bomb • A shot glass of Cointreau® dropped into a glass containing Red Bull®.
Flaming Dr Pepper® • A shot of amaretto is topped with Bacardi 151®, set on fire, and dropped into a glass of lager.

Bomb Techniques

THE HAND METHOD

The most basic way to bomb is like a good fire safety drill: Stop (catch your breath), Drop (the shot into the glass), and Roll (it down your pie hole).

THE BOMB TRAIN

When bombing with friends, this technique makes a splash. (That pun is entirely appropriate.) Line up glasses as shown with one extra empty one. Then balance a booze-filled shot between each one. Knock them over like dominos and then knock them back like dominos filled with booze.

THE BOMB RING

Use the same overly elaborate technique as the Bomb Train but place the glasses in a circle—without the empty one. Knock them over.

THE BOMB BRIDGE

Perfect for sake bombs. The sake shot glass is balanced on two chopsticks over a beer, the table is pounded, the shot glass drops, the mixture is consumed immediately.

Part 2: Fuel

A PARTY ANIMAL CANNOT LIVE ON CHEMICALS ALONE. (Although a few have tried.) Most Party Animals take great joy in all of life's pleasures. Food is no different.

PRE-PARTY EATING

Party Animals have the foresight to maintain a diet during the day that will improve their functioning at night. Their body is their vehicle and this vehicle needs to be running well before they take it off-roading down Barley Lane.

A Party Animal should look for a diet that delivers the following criteria:

Maximum energy · The party lifestyle is a marathon and it needs the right fuel.

Reparative properties · Admittedly the fun of the night does some damage to the rest of the body, so it's best to optimize better choices during the day.

Minimize weight gain · Party Animals need to attract other members of the species. The goal is to keep the beer in the belly—not on it.

3 TIPS FOR BETTER PARTYING THROUGH NUTRITIONAL SCIENCE

1. RESPECT THE MOST IMPORTANT MEAL: Research shows breakfast improves alertness and concentration, helps shed pounds by preventing overeating during the day, and prevents obesity, diabetes, and heart disease. So why is it so damn hard to eat right in the morning? Keep the right foods within arm's reach of the bed or the couch to prevent you for going to a bad place. Yogurt, cereal with skim milk, and whole grain toast with peanut butter all do the trick.

2. GOOD FATS CHASER: Sounds like an oxymoron (like "white break-dancer") but the right types of fat are concentrated sources of energy. Saturated fat (found in foods like meat, butter, lard, and cream) and trans fat (found in baked goods, snack foods, fried foods, and margarines) have been shown to increase the risk of heart disease. Try replacing saturated and trans fats in your diet with unsaturated fat (found in foods like olive oil, canola oil, nuts, and avocados). Nachos anyone?

3. LIKE WATER FOR ROCKING: Dehydration is one of the leading causes of a lack of energy. The leading cause of dehydration? All the shit you put in your body every night. If you're not well hydrated, your body puts its resources into maintaining your water balance instead of into giving you energy to rock. The Institute of Medicine recommends that women get about 11 cups of water from food and drink each day, and men get about 16 cups daily. Luckily, you have the skills for drinking large amounts of fluids. Just put it to use.

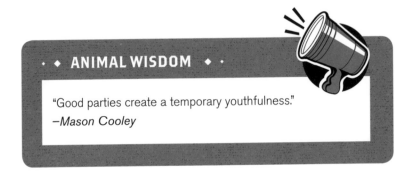

• ◆ ANIMAL WISDOM ◆ •

"Good parties create a temporary youthfulness."
—Mason Cooley

POST-PARTY EATING

The pre-party routine is like a deposit in your health bank, the post-party eating a withdrawal. A greasy, late night withdrawal.

PIZZA

Number one with a pepperoni bullet. Although it originated in Greece and was mastered in Italy, pizza was industrialized in America. Approximately three billion fresh pizzas are sold in the United States every year, plus an additional one billion frozen ones. On average, each person in the United States eats around 23 pounds of pizza every year.

WHY IS IT SO POPULAR?

EASY TO SHARE Not that we recommend Party Animals sharing food. But a pizza is perfectly designed for division and distribution amongst the tribe.

UN-SCREW-UP-ABLE There is great pizza and there is just OK pizza. Did you see that? No bad pizza. Even chain pies can do the deed.

VERSATILITY The pizza is less of a food and more of a platform for food delivery. The crust is like the OS and the toppings are the apps that are designed to fill your recently partied face.

PARTY ANIMAL PIZZA HACKS

COLLECT THE CRUSTS Many people don't like the crusts, or as Party Animals call them, "pizza bones." Call dibs on them early. They can be used for dessert by dipping in icing, as stirrers for Bloody Marys the next morning, or as currency to barter with a hungry hippie.

FREE RIDE HOME If you're at the bar and need a sober lift, just order a pizza from a nearby pizzeria and have it delivered to your house. Catch a ride with the delivery guy.

DEFEND YOUR TERRITORY If you have freeloaders constantly mooching off your munchies, consider sandbagging your next order. Find the topping the moocher dislikes the most—or better yet, is allergic to. Then order extra on your pie. It's like The Club® for your pizza.

THE OLD INSTANT PLATE When the smoldering cheese and lava sauce are burning your hands and staining your carpet, you'll wish you owned plates. But fear not. Simply tear, cut, and gnaw the box into individual pieces to work as plates—for free!

THE SPICE IS RIGHT If the local pizzeria is beginning to know you, take advantage of this relationship to spice up the pizza routine. Ask them to take a page from a New Zealand pizzeria and hide copious amounts of ghost pepper under one unmarked slice. Just one. Now you don't just have a meal—you have a pizza roulette wheel. Whoever gets the pepper piece has to eat that piece and pay for the next pie. Make it hurt in their wallet and gullet.

BURGERS AND FRIES

The term "hamburger" originally derives from Hamburg, Germany's second largest city. And french fries, well, they were invented in Belgium. But it took American ingenuity to bring them together.

WHY IS IT SO POPULAR?

CUSTOMIZABLE Most burgers you can have your way. And at 3 A.M. it's easier than thinking.

UBIQUITY You party out of state and need some late night chow. Over 40 percent of all sandwiches served in the United States are hamburgers, so you know you can always get one.

COMPLETE PACKAGE It's got the protein to power tomorrow's drinking, the carbs to give you the energy to get home, and fat to make sure you don't wither away into nothing.

BURGER AND FRIES HACKS

PIMP YOUR KETCHUP CONTAINER You know those little paper cups that you need twelve of to convey enough ketchup for your fries? They expand, doubling in size and most importantly, condiment capacity.

CROSS THE LINE Millions of Americans have discovered a treat that just a few years ago would have caused uproar in the heartland: They dip their fries into a chocolate shake. For the drunken palate, it combines salty and sweet, hot and cold, starchy and fatty. Some may say, "God created Adam and Eve, not Fries and Shakes." But we invite you to be fry curious and try it yourself.

FRESHEST FRIES FOREVER You are dead set on eating fries and have been looking about the restaurant in anticipation. But when you peep at the fry station, you see a bunch of old, soggy, lonely fries. Here's the solve: Tell them you need to order UNSALTED fries for a reason that you'd rather not talk about in mixed company. They'll begrudgingly make a new batch.

Meet the Douche Burger

In 2012, New York City's 666 Burger food truck created the richest burger on earth. For just $666 you can purchase a foie gras–stuffed Kobe patty covered in Gruyere cheese that's been melted with champagne steam and topped with lobster, truffles, caviar, and a BBQ sauce made with Kopi Luwak coffee beans that have been pooped out by Asian jungle rodents. The whole thing is then served in a gold-leaf wrapper.

STREET FOOD

Don't let the foodie freaks fool you that food trucks are the hot new thing. Eating from the movable contraptions dates back to . . . well, we don't know. But we do know that when leaving a bar at 1:00 A.M., all Party Animals can appreciate having to only stumble a few feet for a tasty eat.

WHY IS IT SO POPULAR?

PROXIMITY Food carts and food trucks represent the shortest distance between you and post-party nourishment.

APPROPRIATENESS The fare on these mobile munchie machines is often perfectly suited for post-party noshing.

UN-KICK-YOU-OUT-ABLE If there is no door, you can't be thrown out of it when you get rowdy with the wait staff.

TOP STREET EATS

DIRTY WATER DOGS An NYC tradition in which skinny hot dogs take a steam bath in some rarely changed water.

FALAFEL Garbanzo bean meatballs with yogurt sauce sounds like a hippie's dream. But a good falafel scratches an itch like nothing else.

CURRYWURST Leave it to the Germans to take a bratwurst and drown it in a sweet and spicy curry sauce. Perfect for post-Oktoberfest feasts.

SONORAN-STYLE HOT DOGS A Mexican spin on the American classic involves a hot dog wrapped in bacon and garnished with everything in the kitchen sink.

FAT SANDWICHES These come from the infamous Grease Trucks at Rutgers University in New Jersey. The groundbreaking Fat Darrell includes chicken fingers, mozzarella sticks, French fries, and marinara sauce on a bun.

Why We Eat Like Shit after a Night on the Piss

BLAME IT ON THE AL-AL-ALCOHOL.

And blame in on your br-br-brain as well. Simply, alcohol messes with how your brain reacts to food. Carefully conducted experiments show that even people who had unwittingly ingested alcohol would end up feeling hungrier and eating more sometime in the following hours.

Other studies have shown that drinking an alcoholic beverage before a meal increases appetite and causes people to eat a bit more than they would otherwise. Last year, a team of researchers from Sussex, U.K., came up with the answer: Alcohol directly interferes with appetite control in your brain. It was found that after alcohol, food actually looked more appealing.

How to Score Free Food

By Chris Barish, Author of *The Book of Bad*

Anyone can pay for a meal—but what's the fun? Here are five ways to chow like a rebel.

CONTINENTAL BREAKFAST. After a long night of debauchery you'll need sustenance to maintain peak performance. At daybreak stroll into a quality hotel walking barefoot or wearing a wet bathing suit so that it appears you are guest who has used the pool. Waltz up to the buffet and help yourself to free plates of the most important meal of the day.

DONUT DUMPSTER DIVE. Score hundreds of free donuts just after closing time—then bring them back to the party and be hailed as a returning hero. Cement your legend with a milk-bong chaser. There are also delicacies to be found in the dumpsters of bagel shops and fast food restaurants.

THE PRACTICAL JOKER. Enter a restaurant, walk up to a table and brazenly eat whatever you want off the patron's plates. After they express their incredulity—and perhaps rage—sheepishly apologize, point to hidden camera that doesn't exist, and tell them it's for a TV practical joke show on MTV4.

BOGUS BIRTHDAY. If you find yourself at a restaurant, tell the hostess or waiter that it's a birthday celebration. Not only will you achieve gratis cake, you'll get the pleasure of watching the staff uncomfortably sing Happy Birthday.

SHOWROOM SAMPLER. To create an aura of class, luxury car dealerships often lay out a well-balanced food spread in the guest area. Get past the oily salesman in the showroom—and his bullshit rap—by telling him you're "only browsing." For free food, that is.

The Party Animal Workout

Guide to Burning Calories

It's tough being a Party Animal. Between all the beers consumed and the pizza stuffed down the gullet, it's very easy to go from svelte to sloth. But, the very best party animals know how to incorporate fat burning workouts into their standard party procedure.

The activities below estimate the average number of calories a 150-pound partier can burn by doing said activities for 30 minutes. These calories are then converted into a standard party unit of measure: a twelve-ounce bottle of warm light beer.

Activity	Calories	Beer Equivalent
SHOOTING POOL Basic billiards without the "Color of Money" lip-synching.	74	
BEER PONG The sport of champions played at a reasonable clip.	128	
DIRTY DANCING Nothing wrong with a little aerobic bump 'n' grind.	77	
TURKEY BOWLING Knocking down a stack of empties with a frozen bird.	82	
KEG TOSSING Tossing an empty barrel around a backyard.	360	
RUNNING FROM COPS Sprinting from the fuzz and hiding in bushes.	578	
SKINNY DIPPING Getting wet and wild without party attire.	154	
RUNNING FROM COPS WHILE NAKED Works the upper body while covering the lower.	626	
CARRYING PASSED OUT FRIEND HOME The burden of the last man standing hangs heavy.	352	
CLEANING UP THE NEXT DAY Piecing together the night and the furniture.	135	

CHAPTER
·· 3 ··

Welcome to the Jungle

PARTY HABITATS

IT IS NO SURPRISE THAT PARTY ANIMALS SPEND much of their time in the party environment.

But like cockroaches or Starbuck's locations, Party Animals have adapted to survive in just about any environment. Can a fish live without water? Can a human exist without oxygen? Can a Party Animal rage without a party? The answer to all these important questions is obvious—no!

Having the proper atmosphere, the proper locations and places, and the proper accoutrements is imperative to sustain not only an acceptable environment but also to encourage a passionate common attitude—exuberance, revelry, merriment, and, dare we say, euphoria.

This chapter will act as your guide through the dense jungle and uncharted territories of the Party Animal Kingdom.

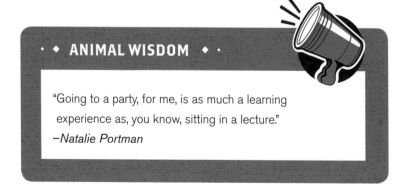

・ ◆ ANIMAL WISDOM ◆ ・

"Going to a party, for me, is as much a learning experience as, you know, sitting in a lecture."
—*Natalie Portman*

PARTIES COME IN ALL SHAPES AND SIZES. And the Party Animal must be able to adapt—like a chameleon of sorts—to the unique environment of each occasion. And knowing the right party term is part of the battle.

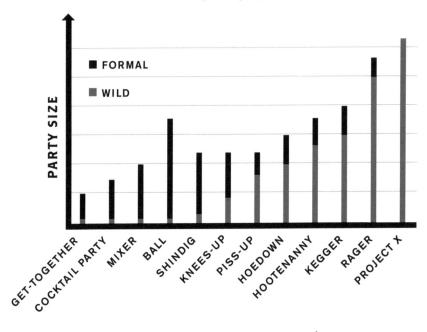

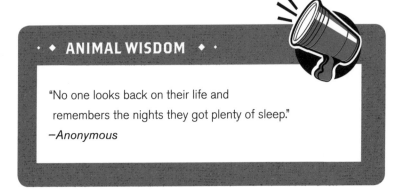

· ◆ ANIMAL WISDOM ◆ · ·

"No one looks back on their life and remembers the nights they got plenty of sleep."

—Anonymous

Get-Together ◦ Small, informal party where everyone is a friend.

Cocktail Party ◦ Slightly larger get-together with a variety of friends and acquaintances, but civilized behavior is still expected.

Mixer ◦ Less-formal party designed to get people to meet each other— so mingling is expected.

Ball ◦ Big, formal party requiring fancy clothes. On the bright side: limos and princesses.

Shindig ◦ Smaller than a ball, but still classy.

Knees-Up ◦ A British term for a shindig with drinking and dancing.

Piss-Up ◦ A British term for a shindig with just drinking.

Hoedown ◦ A large, informal Southern party with a band and dancing.

Hootenanny ◦ A hoedown with even more people and even more drinking.

Kegger ◦ Bigger party, requires a keg as the focus of the night, not as exclusive as a get-together.

Rager ◦ Multiple kegs, no limit to turn outs, possible destruction.

Project X ◦ Based on the movie, this is a house party with a splash of Armageddon.

TO A PARTY ANIMAL, a party night is not one-dimensional. It's like a fine diamond with multiple facets—to be turned, admired, and possibly stolen by a flexible burglar dressed in a black bodysuit.

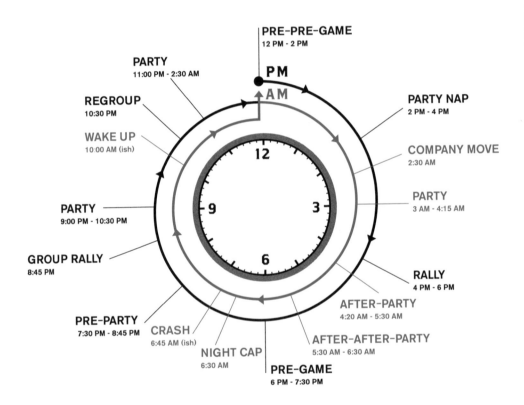

PRE-PRE-GAME
12 PM - 2 PM

PARTY
11:00 PM - 2:30 AM

REGROUP
10:30 PM

WAKE UP
10:00 AM (ish)

PARTY
9:00 PM - 10:30 PM

GROUP RALLY
8:45 PM

PRE-PARTY
7:30 PM - 8:45 PM

CRASH
6:45 AM (ish)

NIGHT CAP
6:30 AM

PRE-GAME
6 PM - 7:30 PM

AFTER-AFTER-PARTY
5:30 AM - 6:30 AM

AFTER-PARTY
4:20 AM - 5:30 AM

RALLY
4 PM - 6 PM

PARTY
3 AM - 4:15 AM

COMPANY MOVE
2:30 AM

PARTY NAP
2 PM - 4 PM

Party Spaces

WHILE PARTY ANIMALS ARE KNOWN FOR migrating great distances for parties, they are particularly adept at creating their own. This nesting behavior happens for temporary occasions and permanent residences alike.

OVERALL PARTY SPACE PRINCIPLES

Choosing the right party space is a talent that most Party Animals possess. They have a six-pack of sixth sense about what makes it right for partying. But upon closer examination, it is clear that several principles are at play.

CLEAN-ABILITY IS KING

Great party spaces are easy to clean so they can be trashed again. No one likes to clean up. But no one likes smell of week-old body funk and pizza either. So the professional partier looks for surfaces that can be wiped, swept, and, ideally, hosed down.

TIGHT IS RIGHT

Conventional wisdom would lead you to think bigger is better. But it would also lead you to believe the McRib was a good idea. The truth is that smaller spaces which compact the energy of the night create a better space for rocking.

DON'T PARTY WITH STRANGERS

A great party space, whether it's an apartment, a tailgate lot, a party boat, or a cow pasture, is only as good as its social context—in other words: the neighbors. Ironically, it's less to do with the surrounding people being like you; it's more about them liking you. The savvy Party Animal knows how to prepare these influential people for the event and take care of anything afterwards.

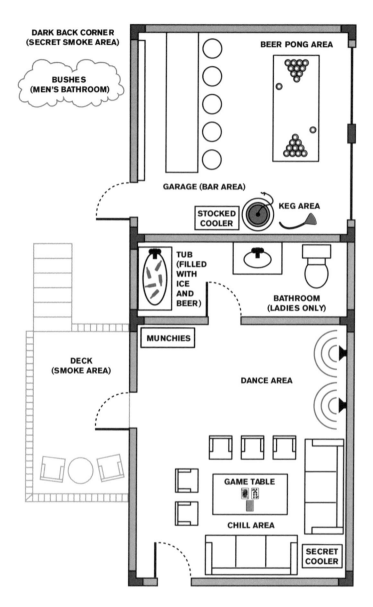

PARTY PAD FLOOR PLAN
1/8" = 1'0" (sort of)

PARTY SPACE ACCOUTREMENTS

To be deemed an official party space, certain criteria must be achieved to meet this highest of standards. A designated space is just the beginning, and filling this space with the essential party accoutrements is what determines the difference between a roof over your head and a roof that's raised and quite possibly on fire.

AMPLE SEATING

First things first: When outfitting the party space, make sure there's enough seating for everyone to relax and take a load off. Couches, futons, chairs, bean bags, tree stumps, whatever, as long as partiers can sit.

BAR AREA

Partiers need to easily find the watering hole. If you can build or buy a legit bar, more power to you; if you can't, a simple folding table with booze on top will do the trick.

DANCE FLOOR

And by dance floor we mean an open area so partiers can dance. This is the easiest of them all: Just leave a space no smaller than 8'× 8' wide open and the Party Animals' instincts will let them know this is where to cut the rug.

HOW TO CLEAN UP IN TWO MINUTES

Quick, "they" are coming over. And they won't approve of the state of your room or apartment or prison cell. Here's how to pull it off.

Focus the forces

Close the doors to all non-essential rooms and put your energy into one prescribed path.

Out of sight

It's not about clean—it's about the appearance of clean. So get clothes, trash, food, farm animals, and anything else out of sight.

Dust and freshen

Take a few handfuls of dryer sheets and use them to wipe down dusty and dirty surfaces.

Clean yourself

If you have *your* stuff together, they'll have less to look around for.

DESIGNATED WEED AREA

It's important to set up a discreet area away from the main gathering place for fellow partiers to partake in some puff without feeling uncomfortable. It doesn't need to be fancy, just inconspicuous and private.

PROFESSIONAL HANDMADE BEER PONG / GAME TABLE

Nothing says, "This is a party space" like a handmade, custom painted beer pong / game table. The time, dedication, and care put into building one of these essentials puts everyone on immediate notice that this is a serious party establishment.

Top Places to Party

THE HISTORIC SUCCESS OF THE PARTY ANIMAL HAS BEEN its ability to adapt to a variety of different environments. Below are several of the most common party places.

Backyards • Where else can you drink while tanning, drink while jumping on a trampoline, drink while grilling, and drink while making fun of the stars? Nowhere else.

Fraternity Houses • These structures have been dedicated to the dark arts of partying for generations.

Party Barges • These pontoon boats are made less for speed and more for speed Quarters (see page 165). When they all come out you get what some lovingly refer to as a redneck yacht club.

Booze Cruises • If Party Barges are like floating living rooms, Booze Cruises are like floating frat houses. They combine the best things in life: the open bar and the open water.

Party Buses • Sure a Party Bus can get you from point A to point B, but in the process you can also add a few points to your blood alcohol level.

Tailgates • Claiming a plot of land and settling it with a feast taps into the primitive Party Animal within. To rock the lot better, see page 94.

see page 94

Infamous Party Pads

Big Boi's Boom Boom Room

Tommy Lee's Party Room with a Freak Swing

The Kennedy Compound

Any *Real World* Location

The Playboy Mansion

BEST NORTH AMERICAN PARTY CITIES

Las Vegas, Nevada • "Sin City." How could you go wrong?

New York, New York • The city that never sleeps—mostly because it's too busy partying.

Miami, Florida • "Looks like this party [puts on sunglasses] already started."

Montreal, Canada • The most rocking city to sport a Maple Leaf flag, Montreal is all "aboot" partying.

Columbus, Ohio • The ultimate college town through and through, this Midwest gem is a party mecca.

BEST INTERNATIONAL PARTY CITIES

Amsterdam, Netherlands • Legalized pot. Need we say more?

Ibiza, Spain • The home of clear water for skinny-dipping in and soft sand for passing out on.

Mykonos, Greece • Lots of wine, olive oil, and wrestling at literally any time of the day thanks to the always open bars.

Rio de Janeiro, Brazil • Beautiful, near-naked people make this a prime city for Party Animals with a streaking preference.

Saint-Tropez, France • A popular celebrity party spot, the French government actually once closed this place down due to the excessively decadent parties.

TOP LEGENDARY PARTIES

Burning Man (Black Rock Desert, Nevada) • One of the biggest bonfire parties of the year. Be cautious of hippies.

Battle of the Oranges (Ivrea, Italy) • Look, you're going to get drunk and throw food, so you might as well do it with thousands of your closest friends.

Oktoberfest (Munich, Germany) • One-liter beers, lots of drunken singing, and pounding on tables. Sounds like the usual to us.

Carnaval (Rio de Janeiro, Brazil) • The only thing hotter than the near-naked parade marchers is the "Are we two inches from the Sun?" heat.

Holi (northern India) • Lots of hugging, lots of rubbing finger paint on each other. It's like kindergarten, but with bhang (it's like a cannabis chai latte).

TOP PARTY SCHOOLS

University of Texas at Austin • The town's motto is "Keep Austin Weird" and the students at UT make sure to live up to those words with "Bigger than Texas" partying.

West Virginia University • WV manages to keep parties going hard despite a fairly lax Greek life, which means more boozing, less spanking.

University of Georgia • The students of Athens, Georgia, have long been known for their partying—not to be confused with the students of Athens, Greece, who are known more for naked Greco-Roman wrestling.

University of California, Santa Barbara • It's a college on the ocean—perfect for skinny-dipping.

Ohio University • Often voted the #1 party school in the U.S.A., most likely because people in Ohio have nothing else to do but party. Works for us!

University of Mississippi • Ole Miss's unofficial motto, "We may not always win the game, but we never lose the party," shows they have their priorities straight.

Penn State University • Just about everyone at this school plays some kind of intramural sport, which means plenty of celebrations and subsequently drinking out of cleats.

University of Florida • Hey, they invented Gatorade™, the ultimate hangover drink. That sums it up pretty well.

Tailgate Parties

By Dave Lamm at TailgatingIdeas.com

The North American Party Animal can't always be confined to the four walls of a fraternity house basement. The call of a wide-open parking lot can sometimes be too great for him to resist. In order to be a true Tailgate Party Animal, one must possess these four essential qualities:

1. PREPAREDNESS

Partying in a parking lot is different than a house party. Modern technology can help the Tailgate Party Animal to be at home away from home: a portable generator, along with a portable satellite to keep an eye on the early games while snorkeling beers in the parking lot.

2. VERSATILITY

Most Tailgate Party Animals associate tailgating with NFL and college football. To be a true Tailgating Animal, one needs to tailgate for events of all varieties, including NASCAR, baseball, and concerts. Girls in short cut-offs and cowboy hats are reason enough to expand your tailgate party repertoire.

3. KNOWLEDGE

Knowledge is king, especially when it comes to tailgating. Knowing which gates open earlier than others, understanding the difference between washer toss and ladder golf, and scouting out the sections that have the short lines for the port-a-johns will go a long way.

4. ATTRACTIVENESS

We're not talking about whether a Tailgate Party Animal looks like an underwear model, but rather his or her ability to attract members of the opposite sex to join the party. A batch of margaritas made with a cordless drill will bring the ladies to your tailgate if the opposing choice is warm Natty Light from those other fools.

Road Trips

MUCH LIKE SOME BIRDS THAT MIGRATE THOUSANDS OF MILES each year, Party Animals also possess the instinct to travel to remote habitats in search of the better party. And much like the walkabout rite of passage for Australian aborigines, a road trip can be considered a ritualistic event that marks a young Party Animal's initiation in the kingdom.

Conducting a road trip is pretty simple: Just get in a car, drive, get out of said car, and do your thing. That said, there are some guidelines to observe.

CARS ONLY

It's called a road trip for a reason, meaning any destination must be reached via car and car only. Otherwise, it'd be called a "water trip" or "air trip" or something.

MUST BE A DESTINATION

The difference between a road tripper and a hitchhiker is their goals, and as a Party Animal, it's pretty obvious what that goal should be.

THE MORE THE MERRIER

One-man road trips are doable, but sound kind of depressing. To make the trip memorable, cram some friends in the car with you.

LEAVE YOUR MARK

How else will people believe you've been there? Take plenty of incriminating pictures, but also make sure you party hard enough to let your destination show that you've been there! Just don't do this with spray paint—kind of illegal, although when has that ever stopped you?

IT IS NO SURPRISE THAT A PARTY ANIMAL SPENDS much of its time in the party environment. The Party Animal lives a mostly nocturnal existence—exploring the wilds of the dark night. Unless there is a tailgate, an early concert, a wake and bake party, a keg and eggs party, a three-martini lunch . . .

BIG DAY PARTIES

One of the few positive things about getting older is that you get to celebrate significant new milestones. From your first birthday to your final wake, each one of these events is accompanied by a party and, if you're lucky, an open bar. Come along as we examine the biggest parties of your life.

NEW YEAR'S EVE

There is no better way to celebrate the past 364 days like partying enough for all of them. Sure it's derided by some as amateur night, but even amateurs need to loosen their shit at least once a year, so embrace them on this sacred night.

PROMS

While not everyone gets lucky, Prom Night still offers revelers an unequaled opportunity to celebrate with old friends, dance up a storm, and discreetly feel your date's boobs while pinning on her corsage.

TWENTY-FIRST BIRTHDAY PARTIES

There are few things more magical than the Party Animal's twenty-first birthday. That's because he has finally reached the age where he can legally drink alcohol, gamble, and buy a handgun. In other words, he can finally party like Charlie Sheen on a Tuesday morning.

WEDDINGS

These extravagant celebrations are still a great excuse to party with friends and family and to watch relatives make drunken passes at each other at the open bar.

WAKES

Wakes typically take place in the house of the deceased and are often lively affairs featuring storytelling, drinking, and eating. In many ways they're just like a regular party, except for the fact there's a dead guy in the corner slowly stinking up the room.

SUPER BOWL PARTIES

Unlike a bar mitzvah or a retirement party, the Super Bowl is something everyone can celebrate every year regardless of age, race, religion, or affiliation with the Detroit Lions.

> **◆ ◆ PARTY FACT ◆ ◆**
>
> Americans typically consume 50 million cases of beer, 90 million pounds of chicken wings, 14,500 tons of chips and 4,000 tons of popcorn on Super Bowl Sunday. Not surprisingly, 6% of all workers also call in sick the next day in what has become the country's largest annual hangover.

BACHELOR/BACHELORETTE PARTIES

The ultimate "Farewell to Freedom" tour, these parties are a chance for the groom to enjoy one last fling before tying the knot and losing custody of his testicles. Or they allow the bachelorette to drink out of penis-shaped straws. These celebrations are usually over-the-top bacchanal affairs featuring booze, pills, costumes, strippers, and, in many cases, an arrest warrant.

MIXER PARTIES

These are parties designed to help singles mingle. These themes give people some gimmicks and tricks to get to know each other—and quite possibly get to KNOW each other later.

T-SHIRT PARTY

Everyone shows up in a plain white T-shirt, grabs a marker, and starts writing on each other's shirts. Great for both getting phone numbers and shaming fellow guests.

MIDDLE SCHOOL DANCE

Wear what you wore in middle school, play music from middle school, and of course, serve punch and brownies. (But since you're all grown up, both the punch and brownies should be spiked.)

TIE & WINE

This is a matchmaking party. Make sure an even number of guests are coming (and know your guests' sexual orientation) and have the guys bring a bottle of wine (or designate one of them if it's a gay couple). As they arrive, match them up and tie them up. They can't be untied until they finish their bottle of wine.

How to Plan a Bachelor or Bachelorette Party

Before you rent the strippers and hire the donkey, there are a few things you should know.

PLANNING THE EVENT

When choosing an activity it's important to consider the personality of the guest of honor as well as the less-honorable guests. After all, just because you enjoy midget tossing doesn't mean everyone else will. Some surefire hits include an outing to a strip club, a day on the links, an organized barhop, a booze cruise, or a night of gambling.

TIMING

Never hold a bachelor or bachelorette party the night before the wedding. Although the groom might not mind if he shows up to church hung over and pantless, his bride most certainly will.

TRANSPORTATION

The only designated driver at your party should be the one with his own limo. Arranging to have professional transportation to each venue will ultimately save you money as well as headaches.

Respect the Four Big Rules

Whatever happens at the party stays at the party. That means no photos, no videos, and no evidence.

Always carry enough money to cover bail.

Don't forget to bring along the two party essentials: a) aspirin and b) plenty of one-dollar bills.

Never badmouth their future spouse. You'll have plenty of time to do that once your friend is actually married.

RUBIK'S CUBE

Wear 3 different Rubik's cube colored items of clothing and trade with people to get all the same color by the end of the night.

THEME PARTIES

CLASSIC TOGA

It's the missionary position of theme parties. But it is a rite of passage for every collegiate American to attend one.

VIKING FEST

Imagine a toga party but with furry costumes instead of flowing robes. That and mead and eating meat off the bone.

BEER-STER EGG HUNT

Everyone gets a basket and must pick up beer cans that have been strategically hidden all around the area. Participants must work fast to compete against each other and the inevitable warming of the beer.

How to Tie a Toga

YOU'LL NEED:
- 1 clean white bed sheet (Queen or King)
- Safety pins
- A toga party to attend

STEP ONE
First, do some laundry so your sheets are clean, stain-free, and don't look like an episode of *CSI* under black lights.

STEP TWO
Drape your sheet over your left shoulder with one corner extending across your lower back. Wrap the rest of the fabric across your chest and tuck it under your right arm.

STEP THREE
Keep wrapping it across your back and then under your left arm. Pull it tight.

STEP FOUR
Bring remaining fabric back across your midsection under your right arm. Tie this corner with the corner hanging against your back from Step Two. Tie a second knot to avoid a wardrobe malfunction. Use a safety pin if you have political aspirations.

STEP FIVE
Adjust as necessary. Use more safety pins to further secure and tighten.

STEP SIX
Take a long hard look in the mirror, and decide what do about underwear later.

PROGRESSIVE PARTIES

Progressive dinner parties were all the rage in the 1950s— people would eat each successive course at a different host's house. Now replace dinner with drinking and the 1950s with right damn now. Here are some examples of parties that keep building throughout the night:

MR. POTATO HEAD PARTY

Everyone in your dorm wears jeans and a plain white T-shirt (that you don't care if it gets written on). Each dorm room has a special drink and something for all of you to add to your wardrobe (e.g., necklaces, fake tattoos, flowers to put in your hair, bow ties). Dress each other up.

GOLF PARTY

Foursomes move from room to room taking different shots and recording them on a scorecard. Needless to say, playing all 18 holes will result in a subpar morning the next day.

AROUND THE WORLD PARTY

Too broke to travel? Why not bring the world to you? Have every room of your house or dorm floor decorated as a different part of the world and offer a specialty drink from that region. One room can be Mexico (margaritas), another room can be Paris (champagne), and another can be Cuba (mojitos).

SEVEN DEADLY SINS PARTY

Lust, Greed, Gluttony, Pride, Sloth, Wrath, and Envy are the seven deadly themes your guests can dress up as at this party. Have each room dedicated to a sin, like the Lust room filled with condoms and the Greed room filled with fake money and poker chips. Once guests enter your version of party hell they must participate in an array of dirty deeds the whole night . . . anything the devilish host commands.

STUNT PARTIES

These celebrations are the polar opposite of casual get-togethers. They take planning, preparation, and quite possibly permits. Below are some of the most infamous ones.

PAMPERS PARTY

Everyone wears diapers. No one uses the toilet. On the plus side, there are no bathroom breaks—just rocking all night. On the negative side, you don't know if someone is peeing while you talk to them.

FOAM PARTY

Fill the party venue with obscene amounts of party foam. A good excuse for minimal clothing. Usually this is at insane beachside dance clubs. But why not bring that buzz to your next house party?

NUCLEAR FALLOUT PARTY

Cover all the walls with black plastic. Replace all of the lights with black light bulbs. Mix a giant aquarium with Gin & Tonic—it glows like a reactor under the black light. Once the reactor is finished, give everyone neon spray paint to coat the walls—and each other.

ABC PARTY COSTUMER IDEAS

Towels So easy, so expected, so don't think you'll be alone.

Duct Tape Clothes Just don't put the adhesive side onto those parts.

Aluminum Foil Good for molding to fit your body, but beware of the microwave.

Strips of Condoms Colorful, sometimes free, always good to keep handy.

Pizza Boxes Plenty of raw materials, you need a box cutter and imagination.

Bacon Strips Woven into Sheets *Top Chef* meets *Project Runway*.

INDOOR BEACH PARTY

This is best executed on the coldest weekend of the year. And go all out. Real sand. Lifeguard chairs. Surfboards. If you really commit, get sunburnt just for the occasion. Put out of your mind the thought of finding sand in every inch of your place for the next nine months.

ABC PARTY (ANYTHING BUT CLOTHES)

You can wear anything on your body as long as it was not intended as clothing. Prizes are given out for the best costumes so competition is fierce. This is a chance to show off your body if you have a good one, or your creative mind if you don't.

YARD PARTY

This party theme also encourages wardrobe malfunctions. The rule for the party is that you must come as a couple. And you can only wear what you can make from one square yard of fabric. One of the best, most devious versions is to assign the couples—pairing the biggest two individuals to test their creativity and the tensile strength of the fabric.

Properly Crashing a Party

IT'S TOUGH BEING THE LIFE OF THE PARTY when your name's not on the guest list. That's why we've created a foolproof guide to crashing any event at any time. From weddings to keg parties, you'll never need an invitation ever again.

DO YOUR RESEARCH

It's essential to find out everything you can about a party before recklessly barging in. Is it a house party, a wedding, a bar mitzvah, a foam party, or a wake? Is it formal or casual? Is it in the afternoon or evening? Will there be strippers, and if so, how many one-dollar bills should you bring along? These are all things you need to know to make the most of your party crashing experience.

ACT LIKE YOU BELONG

Every good host dreads forgetting the name and identity of one of their invited guests. Seize upon this fear by boldly going up to the host the moment you enter the party and offer them a warm handshake. Adding a hearty "It's so lovely to see you again!" will ensure they'll play along out of fear they've completely forgotten who you are. Stay on the offensive and you can never fail.

· ◆ ANIMAL WISDOM ◆ ·

"Spring is nature's way of saying, 'Let's party!'"
—Robin Williams

COME BEARING GIFTS

No host can refuse a guest who comes bearing gifts. Just ask the Three Wise Men. These legendary party crashers gained admittance into one of the hottest soirees on the planet just by bringing tiny little portions of gold, frankincense, and myrrh. The good news is that you don't even have to spend much money, so long as the host doesn't open your gift until long after you've drunk all their imported beer.

MAKE FRIENDS WITH THE BOUNCER

No one can end your evening more suddenly— or painfully— than the party's resident bouncer. That's why it's important to make friends with this knuckle-dragging meathead as soon as you arrive. Try slipping him a few bucks as you enter the premises or send him a free drink as the night goes on. His allegiance can make all the difference between nursing a few free drinks and nursing a few head wounds.

How to Rage Like a Boss

By Mike Krilivsky, Owner and Partner of THROWED

As the creator and promoter of the largest themed parties in the world, Mike Krilivsky of THROWED (ThrowedPresents.com) is here to help you make the most of your next rager.

ABC PARTY If You're Attending: Wear as little as possible, as long as it isn't clothes–literally anything goes! Duct tape, caution tape, plastic wrap, garbage bag outfits are all great options.

If You're Hosting: Be sure to advertise on your Facebook event pages, your Facebook walls, and tweets the various creative ideas you think of to give your fans and friends helpful hints on what to wear. And make sure to hire a photographer for this one.

FOAM PARTIES If You're Attending: Make sure you are DTF: Down To Foam! The ground or foam pit will usually get pretty dirty so wear sandals or old sneakers because they will get destroyed.

If You're Hosting: Make sure you'll be able to make enough foam to fill the room and for it to be even cool enough to be called a foam party. Order online

or physically make the coolest foam canon you can because that will be the main attraction of the night!

BLACK LIGHT PARTIES
If You're Attending: Buy highlighters and smear the liquid all over yourself like a crazed animal–get wild with it, just don't eat it. Wear all white or UV reactive (neon) clothing so you'll basically be glowing.

If You're Hosting: Don't skimp. Buy tons of glowing necklaces to hand out, drape them from the ceilings, and have glow sticks readily available. And make sure to get enough black lights to really make the venue pop.

INDOOR BEACH PARTY
If You're Attending: Pick out your favorite bikini or swimming shorts– and don't forget your sunglasses. Get some suntan lotion (just for smell–you'll be amazed at how many compliments and conversations you start by wearing some). Leave the boogie boards at home: too big.

If You're Hosting: You gotta have the beach balls. Get as many as you can and release them all at once. The bigger, the better the rager!

DRESS THE PART

The key to fitting in is blending in, so be careful not to go over the top. If everyone else is wearing a suit and tie then your powder blue tuxedo is bound to stand out like the sore thumb it is. Play it safe and wear a classic black suit with a tie instead. Who knows, with a sharp ensemble like that you might even score.

SHOW UP FASHIONABLY LATE

The easiest way to crash any party is to show up when it's already in full gear. By turning up two to three hours after the call time, you'll be arriving when the lights are low, the alcohol is flowing, and everyone's defenses are down. Simply emerge out of the washroom and hit the dance floor running.

DON'T BE AN ASS

Getting into the party is only half the battle. The real trick is staying there until the wee hours of the morning . . . or at least until the last available woman has called it a night. You don't have to be a Boy Scout, but it is a good idea to respect your host and their property. Who knows, if you behave well enough you may even get a legitimate invitation next time.

• ◆ ANIMAL WISDOM ◆ •

"As long as you behave well and are willing to dance, people are okay with you at a party."
—*Bill Murray (on crashing parties)*

How to De-stink a Party Pad

A post-party odor can best be described as combination of stale beer, old smoke, ass with hints of BO, wet dog, and plain old stank. And while a Party Animal has a soft spot in her heart for the funk, it has no place in her place the morning after. Here are some quick and cheap suggestions to de-funk in a pinch.

AIR IT OUT

Cracking the windows is the first step to removing the ass-crack smell. Before you do anything else, place one window fan blowing out and another blowing in to create a de-stinking crosswind.

VINEGA-GRRRR

Funny how this fermented juice is so effective at combating the mess left by drinking fermented juices. Dilute white vinegar with water and use it to wash down floors, walls, and passed-out friends. Even put out a bowl to just evaporate in the air.

BAKING SODA

Shake this other white powder all over your place. Carpet, furniture, even clothing. Let it sit for a few hours—or even a day. Vacuum it out, repeat, and begin to breathe easier.

PRETTY BALLS

A nice finishing touch is to use a few drops of vanilla extract on some cotton balls and scatter them around the house. The sweet, innocent smell makes the sin just float away.

CHAPTER
· · 4 · ·

Animal Instincts

·

BASIC SKILLS
AND BEHAVIORS

·

BEING A PARTY ANIMAL IS MORE THAN THE SUM OF ITS PARTS.
It is more than just looking the part and the ingesting of a few choice chemicals. Oh, no. As legendary literary Party Animal F. Scott Fitzgerald noted, "Action is character." He was referring to his latest novel, but he could have been referring to his latest night out.

Behavior is what makes the Party Animal a complete creature, not just a one-dimensional sketch. And that is why this chapter will cover actions that demonstrate the Party Animal's character: how to stand out from the crowd, how to show people a good time, and ultimately, how to bring the party to the next level.

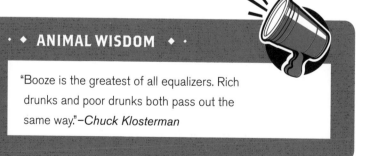

· ◆ ANIMAL WISDOM ◆ ·

"Booze is the greatest of all equalizers. Rich drunks and poor drunks both pass out the same way." –*Chuck Klosterman*

NOT LIKE CARROT TOP, but like any animal in nature looking to maintain its difference, props become the tools to help establish top position in the pack. These props come in two forms: functional rocking and peacocking.

FUNCTIONAL ROCKING PROPS

Like an elite athlete, a Party Animal can achieve a competitive advantage in the awesome department with these accessories.

DRINKING SHOES

This is possibly the single most important piece of equipment for the Party Animal. One's connection to the ground is critical. Ideally, drinking

shoes are comfortable, high traction, clean enough to make it into any establishment, and, of course, free of dog poo.

BOTTLE OPENER

A Party Animal should always have one on her or his person. Key chains are a traditional location for bottle openers. But since keys have a high chance of magically walking away, an expert Animal has a secondary location. Modern technology allows openers to be designed into the soles of shoes, the brims of hats, and the buckles of belts.

BEER GOGGLES

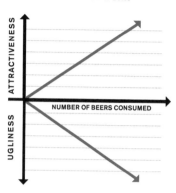

HOW BEER GOGGLES WORK

ATTRACTIVENESS

NUMBER OF BEERS CONSUMED

UGLINESS

Although not technically a physical item, one needs to pay careful attention when the dreaded Beer Goggles do make an appearance. Often unbeknownst to the wearer, Beer Goggles distort your ability to distinguish between a hotty and a notty when approaching a potential sexual partner. Always confirm attractiveness with at least two or three trusted friends, including your club-soda-sipping designated driver.

FRACKET

This is a mash-up of Frat and Jacket but it's not restricted to collegiate parties. A Fracket is a cheap jacket or sweatshirt that provides warmth but is made to get dirty or even lost. If you leave with it, great. If it gets left behind to soak up beer on the floor, great too. It is important to not put valuables in the pockets of the Fracket or it becomes indispensable.

STREAMLINED WALLET

A true Party Animal packs light. And they just carry what they need for the night: I.D., one credit card and some cash. This is not just efficient for the night—it's easier to replace when you inevitably lose it.

How to Open a Beer Bottle with a Lighter

The thinking drinker's method, this approach requires one to apply basic physics equations to unlocking the brew. It needs an object that serves two main tasks: to break the bottle cap's grip and to provide leverage for lifting it off. Here's how to apply it using a lighter:

STEP ONE

Choke up on the bottle with one hand. The gap between your fingers and the lip of the bottle cap needs to be a little less than the width of your lighter.

STEP TWO

Insert the bottom of the lever object between your top finger and the bottom of the cap, aiming above the center of the bone between your knuckle and first finger joint.

STEP THREE

Tighten your grip on the bottle. You should feel one edge of the lighter digging into the flexed muscle between your knuckles on the side of your finger and the other edge should now be pushing up on the bottle cap.

STEP FOUR

Push down on the metal end of the lighter. This will cause the lighter to bend the lip of the bottle cap out away from the beer bottle. If all goes well, the cap will fly off and you will be cool.

SMUGGLING DEVICES

It's a Party Animal's responsibility to ensure that some liquid party be present at every occasion. So they must come packing. Here are a few common methods:

Flask • This classic vessel can be a sophisticated monogrammed silver heirloom or a plastic bottle duct-taped to your thigh.

Beerbelly™ • This ingenious device is a prosthetic stomach that fits under one's shirt and carries 80 ounces of beer—which will, of course, give you a real beer belly.

Winerack™ • Like the Beerbelly for women, this bra contains a plastic bladder for beverages while it lifts and separates.

LOST AND FOUND NOTE

Like the black box on an airplane, you hope you never need to use it. But, when something goes horribly wrong, you'll be glad you did. We've provided a convenient template. Please photocopy, complete, and place in your pocket before leaving your house for the night.

Hello, I'M _____

and I probably partied too hard tonight.

I need to GET HOME TO _____.

PLEASE CALL _____ and tell them to pick me up.

I appreciate your help and hope we can have a drink one day.

If there were a SkyMall™ for Party Animals, it would include these grownup toys.

BUMFLOAT™ · These specially designed floating shorts let you party hands-free from a seated position in the water.

STADIUM PAL® · This special bladder attaches to your leg; the other end attaches to your, um, little leg. This allows you to party without potty breaks.

CRUZIN' COOLER® · Imagine a beer cooler mated with a motorized scooter. Now imagine riding on the back of their offspring. A drinker's dream come true.

GET BOMBED® · This simple molded plastic rack keeps your cups aligned for Beer Pong and helps you carry them to the keg together.

REEF™ **SANDAL WITH BOTTLE OPENER** · When you're chilling out, you want to expend as little energy looking for an opener as possible. Having a sandal that opens beer isn't just lazy. It's genius.

PEACOCKING PROPS

Having a signature thing creates a singular point of difference and generates local star power. This is the immediate magnetism that comes from standing out in the sea of sameness. The key is to choose one or two careful peacocking props to stand out, but not too many props, which will cause you to stand alone—as an outcast.

THE BOOK OF THE PARTY ANIMAL

HEADWEAR

Top Hat (sophisticated)

Sombrero (if you are not Mexican)

Stolen Hat (must have story behind it)

Cowboy Hat (if you are not in the South)

Pimp Hat (if you are not a pimp)

SHIRTS

Ironic T-shirt (ironic)

Intentionally Ugly Shirt (funny)

Intentionally Revealing Shirt (sexy)

Tuxedo T-shirt (classic)

OTHER ACCESSORIES

Oversized Fancy Belt Buckle
(conversation piece)

Pimp Cup (if you are not a pimp)

Animal Hoodie Thing (cute)

Necklace with Giant Clock (yeah, buoy!)

ANIMALS

Snake (risky)

Lizard (exotic)

Ferret (cute)

Cool Dogs (entertaining)

Smoking Monkey (awesome)

AN ODE TO THE OVERLOOKED TIE

Often considered a totem for the stiff corporate world, a simple tie in the hands of the right Party Animal can prove to be quite indispensable, and can have many different applications.

INSTANT HEADBAND

LOVE LASSO

EMERGENCY TOURNIQUET

SLINGSHOT TO HURL STONE AT GIANT

MOUTH GAG

GUITAR STRAP

MAKESHIFT BELT

CLEANING RAG

COIN CLOTH

Lampshade Headgear

FOR THE GENERAL PUBLIC, donning a lampshade at a party has come and gone out of favor. But for Party Animals, it is a universal sign of being the life of the party—and more importantly, it is a tribute to Animals of the past.

It's impossible to pinpoint the original forefather of fun, but it probably started in the early 1900s. Even Charlie Chaplin rocked a shade as far back as 1917 in his film *The Adventurer.* So today, you can carry this torch of good times—well, technically, it's the cover of said torch, but you get the point.

✦ ANIMAL WISDOM ✦

"Stay as long as you want, try to avoid putting any lampshades on your head, because there are a lot of photographers here." *—President Barack Obama to guests on St. Patrick's Day.*

THE BOOK OF THE PARTY ANIMAL

THE CLASSIC

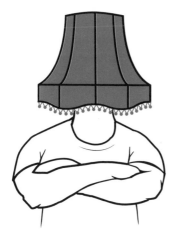

THE SICK PUPPY

THE DUMB DONALD

THE BIG PAPAL

Party Animal Hairstyles

FEW THINGS DEFINE A PERSON as well as their hair. This is equally true for Party Animals, if not more so. Rocking a nice 'do not only tells the crowd that you're here to party, it also lets them know what kind of party machine you really are. Here are a few of the basics:

MALE 'DOS

AFRO

Back in the '60s when the Party Animal movement really started to gain momentum, people let their curls do the talking. Afros became such a necessity to Party Animals that science even found a way to deliver those rocking tight curls to those naturally born without them (hence, chemical perms).

MULLET

Business up front, party in the back. The mullet took the '70s and '80s by storm, becoming the hair equivalent to the "work hard, play hard" style of the lower middle class. Today it is worn ironically in hipster circles. And un-ironically in redneck circles.

MOHAWK

Both a fashion statement and a natural defense mechanism against predators (such as cops and squares), the Mohawk still retains its status as one of the top party 'dos to this day.

BALD

Timeless: A heaping head of hair has never been a party necessity. In fact, the bald look adds a stark minimalist approach to peacocking that almost all Party Animals can appreciate. The true power of the bald head, however, is the invitation to others to rub it for good luck.

FEMALE 'DOS

BIG

Female Party Animals (and particularly long-haired males, for that matter) use the big hairdo to let everyone know they're in the room and even push other partiers out of the way for you—if you used enough hairspray.

CRIMPED

Use the crimped 'do to invoke a lion-like look into your mane. Hey, if you're going to party like an animal, that animal might as well be the king, or queen, of the jungle.

TEASED

Lighthearted and flimsy, the teased look lets everyone in the room know that this is a noncommittal Party Animal: here now, but possibly willing to flock to a better party at a moment's notice.

POOF

Originally called a high bouffant in the late '60s, the poof has recently made a resurgence into the mainstream party scene through modern-day Party Animal Snooki, the queen of peacocking.

Creating a Signature Move

SOMETIMES THE BEST PEACOCKING PROP IS YOURSELF—employ a signature sound, a signature style, and, perhaps most importantly, a signature move. Simple or elaborate, classic or original, clean or obscene, this pose is your visual calling card. To paraphrase that wise philosopher Madonna: Do not remain standing, pose your body, it is quite easy.

1. STUDY THE GREATS

Find inspiration in the most influential "movers" and shakers of our time. Start with Michael Jackson, Elvis, and M. C. Hammer in the world of music, move to LeBron James and Usain Bolt in the world of sports and finish with Henry Winkler and Chuck Norris in the realm of pop culture. Closely observe how each figure executes and replicates their signature moves time after time.

2. GO BIG OR STAY HOME

Small moves tend to get lost in a crowd so make yours as big and bold as possible. Use your body, stretch your limbs, and take up as much physical space as you can without intruding on the space of your fellow partiers.

3. GET CREATIVE

Take a page out of Steve Martin's playbook and use props to make your move pop. Use your drink, incorporate an empty pizza box, or enlist the help of your fellow partiers to transform your move into a truly memorable spectacle.

4. KEEP IT SHORT AND SWEET

Although creating a signature move may take some time, watching it should not. Keep your move short and sweet to ensure maximum impact and to prevent your alcohol-addled audience from losing its focus.

How To Work a Crowd Like a Pro Wrestler

By Kurt Angle, Olympic Gold Medalist and Professional Wrestling Legend

In both pro wrestling and parties, there are many types of psychology to get your fans rumbling and chanting your name. And I've kicked ass in both. The trick is getting the crowd emotionally involved. In the sport we call this fan reaction "Pop." Here's how to get your party (or wrestling career) on and poppin'.

FIRST POP CUE THE MUSIC: Having a signature song to announce your arrival isn't just for kings these days. Pick a track to have cued up before you come in. Then BOOM! Blast it (and any pyrotechnics if you have them), enter the room, and make heads turn.

SECOND POP SIGNAL THE ENTRANCE: As the music rocks the room, stand for a beat and raise your hands high. Stare at the crowd like you're a rock star and they'll react like a rock crowd. Hold it.

THIRD POP PRESS THE FLESH: When you walk into the room, act like you're the baddest dude on the planet while still acknowledging the fans. So give out high fives by the handful as you dominate the crowd.

FOURTH POP RALLY THE CHANT: The crowd needs to know that you need them too. So step up to any formidable challenge and take on the heat. It could be a game, an off-the-roof belly flop or, in my case, a huge sweaty opponent. And get the crowd chanting your name. They become part of the experience, and you become more awesome by the second.

FIFTH POP BREAK OUT THE MOVE: To have the crowd lose their minds, you need a signature move. In the ring, mine is the feared ankle lock. Yours might be a power flex, a quick dance move or whatever the hell you want to do. Just do it and do it often to get the crowd into a frenzy. Remember: God gave them faces–it's your job to melt them off.

IF YOU ARE AMONG THE MANY, many people who are clueless about shaking your groove thing, there's nothing to worry about. Here are some proven dance moves for Party Animals of all ethnicities.

THE PELVIC THRUST

Moving one's moneymaker to the rhythm is a go-to dance move everyone can agree on.

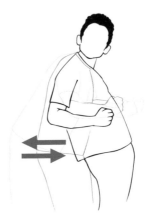

THE THRILLER

With the recent resurgence in popularity of zombies, it's the perfect time to break out this MJ classic.

THE RAISE THE ROOF

For the uncoordinated, this move only requires an upper body motion to the beat.

THE POGO

For the uncoordinated, this move only requires a lower body motion to the beat.

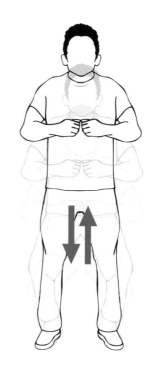

THE POP-N-LOCK

This breakdance classic is always a showstopper—and occasionally a nose-breaker.

THE FIST PUMP

Born on the Jersey Shore, this move is about beating the beat back—and showing off your guns.

Songs with "Party" in the Title:

"(YOU GOTTA) FIGHT FOR YOUR RIGHT (TO PARTY)" – Beastie Boys

"PARTY PARTY PARTY" – Andrew W.K.

"GROVE ST. PARTY" – Waka Flocka Flame

"IT'S A PARTY"– Busta Rhymes

"IT'S MY PARTY (AND I'LL CRY IF I WANT TO)"– Lesley Gore

"PARTY"– Beyonce

"DEVIL'S PARTY"– INXS

"GET THE PARTY STARTED"– P!nk

"MY KINDA PARTY" – Jason Aldean

"PARTY ROCK ANTHEM" – LMFAO

"PARTY"– Boston

"PARTY IN THE U.S.A."– Miley Cyrus

"PARTY UP (UP IN HERE)" – DMX

"THE PRINCE OF PARTIES" – Flight of the Conchords

"PARTY HARD"– Andrew W.K.

"PARTY AND BULLSHIT" – The Notorious B.I.G.

"PARTY ALL THE TIME"– Eddie Murphy

"LIFE OF DA PARTY"– Snoop Dogg

"THE PARTY'S OVER"– Wille Nelson

"PARTYMAN"– Prince

"PARTY ALL NIGHT"– Quiet Riot

"(LET'S HAVE A) PARTY"– Elvis Presley

"I DON'T WANT TO SPOIL THE PARTY" – Beatles

"DANCIN' PARTY"– Chubby Checker

"DON'T STOP THE PARTY" – Black Eyed Peas

"SOUL SHAKEDOWN PARTY" – Bob Marley and the Wailers

"DO YOU WANNA GO PARTY" – KC & The Sunshine Band

"PARTY ON THE PATIO"– ZZ Top

"HERE FOR THE PARTY" – Gretchen Wilson

"I WANNA ROCK-N-ROLL ALL NIGHT (AND PARTY EVERYDAY)"– KISS

"DEAD MAN'S PARTY"– Oingo Boingo

Banging Your Head

HEADBANGING HAS ALL OF THE RHYTHMIC WILD ABANDON of dancing but without the lateral movement. While it originated with the heavy metal of the early 1970s, it has extended to just about every form of music and every form of party. So it's even more critical to know the basics of bang.

1. TUNE THE INSTRUMENT

Center your head and neck and attempt to find the neutral neck posture where it is straight and relaxed. Then slowly turn your head to each side as well as up and down. Hold each side for 20 to 30 seconds. Rolling your neck could cause injury—as will headbanging itself.

2. BUILD FROM A FOUNDATION OF ROCK

Plant your feet firmly on the ground—slightly farther than shoulder width apart. Stagger your feet with your dominant foot six inches forward and your other foot six inches back. Now bend your knees as you place approximately 57 percent of your weight on your front foot.

3. GROW LONG HAIR

Admittedly this may take more time and commitment than currently available, but long hair provides more wind resistance, more rhythmic pendulum action, and ultimately, more awesomeness.

THE BOOK OF THE PARTY ANIMAL

4. BEGIN THE BANGING

Most headbanging takes places along a single vertical axis, so maintain a singular directional plane. The movement along this plane is dictated by the music: slower songs demand a longer arc of movement; faster songs require a shorter speed-bang form.

Try not to move your head more than 43 degrees to ensure your head does not fall off your body like a broken PEZ© dispenser.

5. USE YOUR HANDS

Don't let the name "headbang" fool you, it involves the whole body—especially the hands. Consider using yours to pick up an air guitar, flash the devil horns, punch the air, or just hold on to something for dear life.

6. TAKE A NIGHT OFF

You will undoubtedly feel sore from this activity, so make sure to rest your neck the next day. Do not headbang or nod in agreement to anything for at least 24 hours. If that makes sense, just tap your foot twice.

Spraying Champagne

THERE WAS ONCE A TIME when champagne was a revered liquid, only to be enjoyed daintily from a fluted glass with the occasional upturned pinky. No more. Thanks to post-game celebrations and rap videos, it's now more likely to be sprayed than sipped.

1. READY

The first part is easy: Remove the foil and the wire hood. Now, the next part is even easier: Simply do not shake the bottle. Unless you want to tempt fate and risk premature popping, leave it unshaken.

2. AIM

The equation is the higher the position, the greater coverage, distance, and circumference. So take the high ground and stand on your chair, climb up onto the bar, or join the dancers on stage. Make sure you can aim above the heads of the crowd members—not directly in their faces.

3. HOLD ON NOW

While keeping the bottle as un-jostled as possible, gently remove the cork and place your thumb on the top of the bottle. Apply enough pressure to ensure your thumb completely covers the opening.

4. FIRE

When the right song comes on—or your team officially wins the game— release the kraken. Pre-pump with three to four shakes to build up more pressure. Move your thumb to expose about one quarter of the opening and let the bubbly goodness out. Keep shaking steadily to maximize distance.

5. SHARE THE WEALTH

It is just plain rude to focus on one person—regardless of their social stature. Or physical stature. Spread the spray around the room and not just on the hotties in the front row.

Swinging From Chandeliers

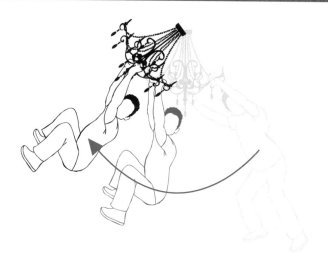

SWINGING FROM A CHANDELIER is a well-trodden euphemism for wild parties or wild sexual exploits. Good times either way.

1. MAKE SURE YOU CAN LIVE WITH THE DAMAGE

Most likely the chandelier will break and pull drywall and wiring with it. So ensure that the house is not yours. Or anyone's you need to impress.

2. MAKE SURE YOU CAN LIVE FROM THE DAMAGE

Chandeliers are made of glass, metal, and occasionally other sharp stuff. And, as pointed out above, it will probably fall on you. So try to choose one with as few damaging parts as possible.

3. LIFT LEGS UP, NOT OUT

Do not extend your legs like you are on a trapeze. Simply bend your legs and bring them to your chest. This creates less of a pendulum effect that, again, puts more force on the fixture.

4. DISMOUNT WITH EXAGGERATED FLAIR

You may not be a prepubescent gymnast winning a gold medal for your country and demanding yet lovable coach, but you can land like one. Thrust your arms up, your butt out, and your smiling grill in everyone's face.

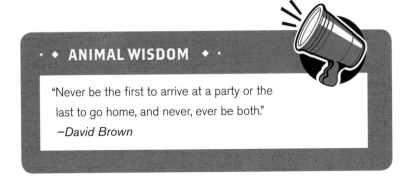

· ◆ ANIMAL WISDOM ◆ ·

"Never be the first to arrive at a party or the last to go home, and never, ever be both."
–*David Brown*

Making a Splash

PUTTING A PARTY ANIMAL IN THE VICINITY of a body of a water is a recipe ... for awesome. For most of the population, pools offer a cool solace from the elements. For the Party Animal, it offers so much more.

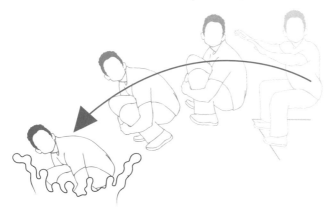

1. CHECK THE ELEVATION

Be certain it is deep enough so that you avoid injury. A general rule is never to jump into water that is less deep than you are tall. Never dive in headfirst: You don't throw off much of a splash, and you could die.

2. PICK A SIDE

The Party Animal has two real choices for pool splashing attire—fully clothed or fully unclothed. Both have pros and cons. It's important to think about what you feel comfortable with—and do the opposite.

3. CREATE A RUNWAY

Walk back about 10 to 15 feet from the pool. If the area is free of objects and people, back up away from the edge leading to the water as far as possible and take a running start. While jumping off a roof or balcony seems much cooler—don't do it. It also could kill you.

4. ALWAYS CANNONBALL

Size of the splash is not from the initial hit, but from the jet of the water that is created after the impact. (This is why belly flops produce more pain than puddles.) The more spherical the projectile the better, so make your body compact and tight. And try to enter the water at as close to 90 degrees as possible.

5. RALLY THE CROWD

After you've surprised everyone by jumping in and creating a spectator-soaking tsunami, it's important to encourage everyone to jump in. A best practice is to bet someone that if you jump in first that they will follow. Social Proof theory in psychology would dictate that people are much more likely to jump in after two people get wet than after just one.

6. CONSIDER PERFORMANCE ENHANCING SUBSTANCES

Physicists have shown that the splash can be enhanced even further when the object (psst, that's you) is covered in a hydrophobic substance. And that includes wetsuits or even petroleum jelly. So consider stripping down, lubing up, and making the most memorable entrance ever.

Making an Exit

STUDIES OF HUMAN BEHAVIOR SHOW that people are more prone to remember the last part of an experience—even more than the beginning. So don't focus on your grand entrance without thinking about your grand exit.

1. **The Lou Gehrig Farewell Speech** ◆ Get everyone's attention, take off your hat, and thank everyone for their support and their alcohol. Choke back some tears—and beers.

2. **The Def Comedy** ◆ Hold a beer bottle or full cup of your favorite beverage above your head. Dramatically drop it on the floor and exit stage left.

3. **The Swayze** ◆ Just be a ghost. One moment you're at the party. Then poof, peace out.

4. **The Irish Exit** ◆ Like The Swayze, but preceded by more drunken revelry. The life of the party one minute, missing in action the other.

5. **The Mayor** ◆ Shake hands, kiss babes, and make sure everyone gets one last good impression before you peace out.

6. **The Company Move** ◆ A true test of a leader, this exit involves bringing a majority of the party with you as you relocate to a B.B.D (Bigger Better Deal).

CHAPTER
· · 5 · ·

Pack Mentality

·

ADVANCED
SOCIAL SYSTEMS
·

PARTY ANIMALS NOT ONLY SHARE A PACT TO PARTY but also share the need to party in packs.

The hard truth is that if you party alone, you have some major issues that this book will not help you with (but an intervention might). What we can help you with, however, is how to properly party hard with your chosen tribe. It may seem simple (get together with friends and have a good time) but in reality, Party Animals must interact within an advanced social system. It has been studied for centuries, but sociologists, archeologists, anthropologists, and all other ologists have yet to fully understand the Party Animal Social System Of Unique Tendencies (P.A.S.S. O.U.T).

But we're here to help set the record straight. For the first time in the Party Animal's chaotic history, we are about to catalog and explain the byzantine social activities that embody all imbibers. In order to preserve and grow the Party Animal kingdom, we must first understand how the kingdom actually works.

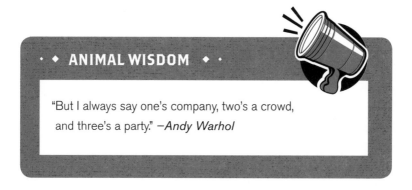

· ◆ **ANIMAL WISDOM** ◆ ·

"But I always say one's company, two's a crowd, and three's a party." —*Andy Warhol*

ONE OF THE MAIN REASONS BEHIND the Party Animal's survival is that they live by the code of the pack, a.k.a. the posse. This pack mentality of extreme loyalty and allegiance to the group is what binds all Party Animals together as a unit—the pack comes before the individual. Pack size and behavior within a pack often vary across species, but the organization follows the same guidelines.

ESTABLISHING PECKING ORDER WITH YOUR CREW

The complex dynamics of the Party Animal crew typically consists of three to seven Party Animals led by an Alpha, followed by an interconnected supporting cast.

THE ALPHA

The Alpha Partier takes the reins of the entourage. This ranking is typically based on experience, popularity, and the strength of their party skills and abilities. The Alpha is your local celebrity and lets everyone know that the pack is well connected. They are known to dominate any party situation and call the shots within their crew—where to meet, where to party, when to leave, who gets to eat the last Jell-O® shot.

THE BETAS

These sidekicks are second in command. The Betas are like scouts— they find out where the party's at, who will be there, and make recommendations to the Alpha. Each Beta often has a particular and valuable skill that helps strengthen the entourage as a unit—not limited to: good looks, humor, enforcement muscle, amazing beer pong skills, etc. If the Alpha becomes too weak (or inebriated) to lead the pack, one of the Betas will take command and lead the posse through the rest of night.

THE OMEGA

The Omega is basically the designated driver for the night and is responsible for the remedial tasks of acquiring the booze and other party treats. This role is often time-shared among the Betas, each taking a turn. This role is actually one of the most important ingredients to the entourage, as they often deal with all mundane tasks like getting the late-night snacks and are responsible for the safety of the overall pack.

THE PHI

Scholars connect the Greek letter Phi to the male phallus. And every group needs a dick. Being a dick means stopping groupthink—the insidious practice of everyone thinking the same damn thing. A dick, like a court jester, becomes the "No Man"—serving as a licensed fool and calls 'em like he sees 'em. The Phi can keep it real when it comes to potential hooks ups ("Not as hot as you think") potential fashion choices ("Nice headband, douche") and potential threats ("This biker party is lame, let's jet").

MASTER BETAS

The Betas are specialists who do different things in the crew. Here are some examples:

The Social Director
Organizes the plans for the night.

The Fixer
Gets the crew out of trouble and can spot trouble before it happens.

The Music Director
Always has the right tunes for any situation.

The Bodyguard
Protects the other members from getting jumped.

The Hook-up
Gets into any party or club, finds tickets to the sold-out concert, the best weed, etc.

HOW TO ROLL WITH A POSSE

WHAT DO YOU CALL YOUR POSSE?

Entourage	Horde
Pack	Gang
Homies	Throng
Crew	Army
Troops	Zoo
Herd	Unit
Gaggle	Coterie

What's the use of having a posse if you don't take it out for a leisurely roll? A Party Animal must know how to move in proper posse formations.

THE RESERVOIR DOG
Makes you feel cool, especially with the soundtrack in your head.

THE FLYING V
The best way to make your way through a crowd on the way to the bar or an impending dance-off.

THE ROLLING DEEP
When you need someone to protect your neck or blow through your life savings, mount up thusly.

THE PACK OF MONKEYS

This formation usually happens during the walk home after a night on the town. Expect to lose one or two posse members along the way.

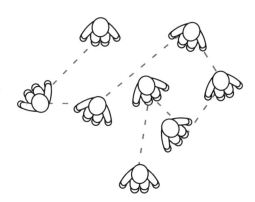

THE NICKNAME ECONOMY IS IMPORTANT to all Party Animals. Earning a nickname (or *nom de fête*) signifies one's acceptance into the tribe. Giving out a nickname signifies one's leadership of the tribe. But like many things in a Party Animal's life, there are rules of engagement.

NICKNAME COMMANDMENTS

I. THOU SHALL NOT SELF-PROCLAIM ONE'S OWN NICKNAME

Like other taboos in culture, this should be strictly avoided—and violators should be subject to scorn and humiliation. This includes the indirect—but equally vile—practice of campaigning for a nickname with others.

II. THOU SHALL NOT JACK ANOTHER'S NICKNAME

As *Reservoir Dogs* taught us: Everyone wants to be Mr. Black. But, like *The Highlander* taught us: There can be only one. If you know of another person currently owning a nickname you have just earned, you must report it to the authorities.

· ◆ ANIMAL WISDOM ◆ ·

"I could party in a cardboard box with people who are funny and don't care. For me, it's really about who I surround myself with, so I just try to always be with hilarious people." —*Ke$ha*

III. THOU SHALL NOT ALLOW "THE" TO BE USED IN A NAME

The reality series *The Jersey Shore* showed a certain East Coast species of Party Animals in their natural environment—and in unnatural shades of orange. But the negative side is that "The Situation" caused this naming structure to fall out of favor. Sorry, Edge.

IV. THOU SHALL RESPECT THE GRANDFATHER CLAUSE

Nicknames are like a buffet: first come, first served. It's important to respect those who were served first. So if a childhood friend knows you as Billy Bed-wetter, you are forbidden from demanding that he refer to you as Billy Badass.

V. THOU SHALL NOT DENY YOUR ORDAINED NICKNAME

The bequeathing of a nickname is a process out of your control. But when the universe has spoken and you become "Tube Sock" you must reply to your new name—and never, never pretend you didn't hear it.

150 Pre-Approved Nicknames

Ace	Butt Nugget	Dutch Dolphin
Action Jackson	Butterbean	Dutch Oven
Admiral Fuckwit	Buttsnacker	Earthquake
All Night Long	Cannonball	El Presidente
Armadillo	Captain Fantastic	El Toro
Bacon Bits	Captain Hoochie	Esquire
Big Daddy	Chocolate Thunder	Flounder
Big Game	Choo-Choo	Flying Beaver
Big General	Chuckles	Four Flusher
Big Hoss	Clutch	Frosty
Birdman	Coach	Fudge Nozzle
Bitmap	Commander Cody	Geezer
Blackbeard	Cool Whip	General Mayhem
Bomber	Crazy Legs	Gizmo
Boner	Creeper	Good Times
Boobie	Crib Midget	Gorilla
Boom Boom	Crotchknuckle	Grand Slam
Boon	Danger Boy	Happy Jack
Boss Man	Dark Horse	Hightower
Brick House	Diesel	Hoagie
Bubba	Dime Bag	Hot Rod
Buckshot	Driller	Howitzer
Bulldog	Dropkick	Hurricane
Bullet-Proof	Drunk Tank	Ironhead
Bullhorn	Dusty	Jellybean

Junkyard Dog	Ol' Red Eyes	Snake Eyes
Kill Switch	Otter	Spud
Kingfisher	Pants Down	Sugar Tits
Knuckles	Paper Tiger	Sunny Jim
Legend	Paydirt	Swags
Lifeline	People's Champ	Sweets
Lizard King	Pinto	T-Bone
Lunchbox	Plugger	Tank
Maestro	Pookie	Teabag
Manimal	Porkchop	Thrasher
Maverick	Pumpkin Head	Thunder Dan
Meat	Red Light	Torch
Midas	Rim-Wrecker	Tough Nut
Moochie	Ripper	Tube Steak
Mookie	Sgt. Slobber	Tuna Can
Moonshine	Shart King	Turbo
Motormouth	Sheep Teats	Turd Blossom
Mr. Fabulous	Shockwave	Turtlehead
Mr. November	Shooter	Twinkle Toes
Mr. Pipeline	Short Fuse	Viper
Nacho	Skunk	Wet Spot
Next Round	Slippery Eel	White Chocolate
Night Monkey	Sloth	Wild Bill
Night Ninja	Slum Dog	Wrecking Ball
Night Train	Snaggletooth	Zeus

WELCOMING A FELLOW PARTY ANIMAL is like welcoming free beer: it just makes you happy. Within the kingdom there are various ways to greet one another and here is the full spectrum of greeting options, depending on the occasion.

FIVES

HIGH-FIVE

Made popular in the sporting world, this basic greeting, with each person raising one hand to slap the raised hand of the other, is a simple yet effective way to punctuate getting the party started.

GIMME SOME SKIN

A symbol of the urban community of the 1970s, this simple yet effective greeting is done with a graceful, smooth palm-to-palm slap then slide. This technique is beloved by both jazz musicians and six-year-olds.

DOUBLE FIVES

Employ all four hands to this kick-up-a-notch version, which can also be used as a celebration after performing an impressive party skill. Great for fans of a team that just scored, or a post-coital couple.

THE DOUBLE DOWN LOW

Also known as the May-Walsh Olympic Clap-Clap, this high-end greeting involves a double High-Five followed by a double Low-Five. Ending it with a bikini-to-bikini full-body hug is purely optional.

THE ORIGIN OF THE HIGH FIVE

The birth of the High Five is a matter of great debate among scholars and barstool philosophers alike, with each camp championing its own founding father. And while there's merit to many of the theories floating around, we believe Glenn Burke, a former Major Leaguer who played for the Los Angeles Dodgers and the Oakland A's in the late 1970s, made this gesture mainstream.

Although the game wasn't broadcast on TV, it was seen by 46,000 fans, many of whom instantly began mimicking it in the stands. Other Major Leaguers also picked up on the manly salute and before you know it, the high five was spreading across America faster than herpes at a swinger's party.

THE CUP

This maneuver is the modern day evolution of the standard Five. The approach is horizontal rather than vertical, with the hand held in a "c" formation with the thumb extended. Clasp hands and hold for a beat or two. It's important that the sound be sharp and hollow—a sign of a proper greeting.

BUMPS

THE CHEST BUMP

Bumping chests is the Party Animal's version of a gorilla beating its chest—it's a sign of strength and dominance. Although chest bumps can be seen as aggressive, they are actually the highest form of respect within the kingdom.

THE FIST BUMP

An understated greeting used by jazz musicians, reggae artists, Stephen Colbert, and other people cooler than us.

THE CUP-TO-BUMP

This action is a symbol of a strong bond between partiers. Start with the basic Cup and then hold the grip and pull into a quick shoulder bump. For emphasis add a quick back slap but do not hold for any longer than one second.

HISTORY OF THE CHEST BUMP

Man has always been fascinated with chests, so it was only inevitable that the high five would eventually morph into a more mammarian celebration. By all accounts, this primal practice first began in December, 1991, when Los Angeles point guard Magic Johnson bumped chests in mid-air with Bryon Scott following a particularly spectacular basket.

Hugs

THE PARTY GIRL HUG ◆

This hug begins several feet away when both parties make eye contact.
Next is a high-heel shuffle run followed by a high-pitched scream that
continues through the actual hug—and sometimes through the whole night.

THE MAN HUG ◆

Also known as the Dude Hug, the Homie Hug, and the Thug Hug, this manly
greeting combines a handshake and a one-armed hug. It is critical that the
hug hand stays in motion—giving both a hug and a hit that tempers any
appearance of romantic affection.

THE AVALANCHE HUG ◆

Usually between two or three good friends who have been partying all
night, this hug starts as a sizable full-body hug. Then it lasts. And lasts.
And lasts . . . The awkward length is finally broken by everyone losing balance
and toppling over.

THE GROUP HUG ◆

As the Party Animal elevates the party, the individuals of the group begin to
act—and drink—as one. This interconnected convergence of positivity is best
illustrated by the group hug. Several people lock arms—holding the shoulders.
Swaying together to music is optional but hard to resist.

Inspiring the Pack

PARTIES ARE ORGANIC ENTITIES that inevitably ebb and flow as the night wears on. When a good party goes bad—and they often do—it's up to the resident Party Animal to resuscitate the flagging event by delivering an inspirational speech. Learn how to breathe life back into any party (yes, even a bat mitzvah) with these helpful tips.

SPEAK FROM THE HEART

Before choosing to follow you, a crowd needs to know that you believe that you're willing to drink your own spiked Kool-Aid®. Speak your message with conviction and sincerity. As comedian George Burns once said, "Sincerity is everything. If you can fake that you've got it made."

PACE AND GESTICULATE

Watch any sports film closely and you'll notice that coaches never remain stationary when delivering an inspirational pregame pep talk. Instead, they gesticulate like they forgot their Ritalin and pace around like caged animals. Their quick, feral, ADHD-inspired movements help build up the tension in the room and give added weight to every utterance, no matter how banal.

DEDICATE YOUR EFFORT

Everyone wants to believe in something bigger than themselves. That's why Hollywood films are full of heart-wrenching moments where teams are asked to push themselves for the sake of a dying or dead teammate. Find someone in your own circle (preferably someone not in immediate danger) whom you can rally around and dedicate your endeavor to their memory.

REFERENCE GREAT MOMENTS IN HISTORY

Like a Journey song, history is full of inspiring moments. It's up to you to draw upon these dusty old gems and remind your audience of how great men have overcome empty kegs and sausage parties in the past and that your crew can do the same. It's not unlike what Bluto said in *Animal House*: America didn't give up "after the Germans bombed Pearl Harbor." Use the grit and gusto of past Party Animals to get your audience off their asses to accomplish the impossible.

CHALLENGE YOUR AUDIENCE

Nothing inspires an audience to take action faster than questioning their Party Animal–hood and referring to them as "a bunch of lames." The prospect of losing face in front of their peers will give them all the inspiration they need to jump into the fray.

CHANT SHEET

A whole is greater than the sum of its parts and these parts need some encouragement. Here are five simple cheers you can start today.

DRINK! DRINK! DRINK!

GO! GO! GO!

PAARRTY! PAARRTY!

USA! USA! USA!

TAKE IT OFF!

KEEP IT BRIEF

Large crowds tend to lose interest after a few minutes—particularly when the alcohol is flowing—so it's crucial to deliver your message as quickly and efficiently as possible. In general, a good inspirational speech should be like a woman's dress: long enough to cover the subject, but short enough to be interesting.

Instant Rally Speech Maker

It's not always easy to get a tribe to step up and make that roadtrip, head to a better party or get back in line for more food at the buffet. So to help, here is a simple motivational speech template.

There comes a time in every _____ life when your
(MAN'S OR WOMAN'S)
_____ is tested; when you discover if you're _____ or a
(NOUN)   (MAN OR WOMAN)
_____. Gang, this is one of those times. We've been together
(ANIMAL)
for _____ years and _____ campaigns and we've suffered
(ADJECTIVE)   (ADJECTIVE)
our fair share of _____. But _____, we've never given up!
(NOUN)   (MILD SWEAR WORD)
We've taken our _____, our _____, and our _____ and we've
(VERB)   (VERB)   (VERB)
risen up off the _____ each and every time. Why, I remember
(NOUN)
back in _____ when we went up against a group of
(LOCATION)
_____. We were _____, undersupplied and
(PROFESSION, PLURAL)   (ADJECTIVE)
outnumbered _____ to one. Who could forget when _____
(LARGE NUMBER)   (FRIEND'S NAME)
went into the fray, yelling, "_____"? Or when
(1980'S TV CATCHPHRASE)
_____ took down _____ men with his bare
(SECOND FRIEND'S NAME)   (NUMBER)
_____? Well, _____ and _____
(PART OF ANATOMY)   (FIRST FRIEND'S NAME)   (SECOND FRIEND'S NAME)
aren't with us today, but I know for damn sure they'd want us to

give it everything we got. So who's with me? It's a _____ day
(ADJECTIVE)
to _____, but it's an even better day to _____!
(VERB)   (VERB)

AS DISCUSSED EARLIER, the Party Animal is an endangered species. Some theorize that this is due to the Party Animal's tendency to perform many a "party foul" (i.e., a faux pas), an act that can easily get you ejected from a party. Fortunately, party fouls are like bowel movements: Everyone has them—some just happen to stink more than others.

COMMON FOULS (FROM LEAST TO FOULEST)

Screwing with the tunes • Some people spend more time picking party music than planning the party. People know this, and they hate the guy who screws it for everyone else.

Announcing your inebriation • Nobody cares that you're drunk, let alone how drunk you are. Stop telling everyone, "I'm so wasted!!"

Spilling • Spillage is the careless act of spilling and therefore wasting alcohol, the lifeblood of the party. Keep to a minimum and you should be all right.

Clogging the toilet • The second it becomes a party, the bathroom becomes a communal washroom. Don't ruin that by using too much T.P.

Not having enough booze • You invited these Animals over, make sure you have enough to keep them happy with that decision.

Raiding the fridge / private stock • If it were meant to be eaten / drunk, it'd be on the table with the rest of the refreshments.

Walking through screen door • The party equivalent of a fly wandering into a spiderweb. Consequences can be equally as dangerous to your reputation.

Falling • Nothing says, "I can't handle drinking" like having your feet give up on you. Even worse on the stairs.

Knocking over the beer pong / flip cup table • If you don't understand the danger in this, you don't deserve to be partying.

Passing out too early • The first person to pass out is like the ball dropping on New Year's Eve; it means the beginning of the end of the party. Don't be the person to start that ugly trend.

Breaking furniture • Not only is this a rude way to thank your host, it's also bound to make at least three people scream, "Hey! I was going to crash there!"

Fighting • Nobody likes a dick, and dicks almost always start fights. Therefore, everyone thinks you're a dick.

Not making it to the bathroom before you puke • Hey, people have to party here, don't cover the place in puke because you can't handle your booze.

Not making it to the bathroom before peeing • See above.

Crotch blocking • If you see people hooking up at a party, let them be. On the other side of the coin, if you're going to take things past heavy petting, then see the next item . . .

Getting busy in someone else's bed • There's nothing grosser than knowing some strange people rubbed their naked junk all over the place where you sleep.

Stealing • After a few drinks, some people think they're Danny Ocean and begin stealing shit. Not cool.

VIOLATION PUNISHMENTS

Tolerance varies as much as personal alcohol tolerances; but the general rule is three strikes and you're out. And the concept of throwing someone "out" is an enactment of one of the bans below.

Local Bans • If the violations are all in one area of the party, then a ban on that area is put into effect. Three drinking fouls, you're cut off. Three pot fouls, you're out of the smoke circle. Three falling fouls, you're banned from standing.

Global Bans • If your fouls are dramatic and cut across areas of the party, you can be thrown out of the whole party. At a bar, this responsibility goes to the bouncer. A house party, the responsibility goes to the biggest friend of the party host. Getting your ass thrown out is bad but not as bad as . . .

Lifetime Bans • These are rare but legendary: a complete ban from partying with that tribe. This is a fate worse than death for a Party Animal, so it should be avoided at all costs.

Party Animals thrive on relationships. Part of the messy complicated world of human relationships is mending a broken one. If a Party Animal is doing her job right, there will be plenty of messy situations to repair. It all starts with a proper apology. Whether you ate someone's grinder or bump-and-grinded with their date, it's a Party Animal's job to keep things right with the pack. Here's several steps for effective sorry saying.

ONLY THE STRONG SAY SORRY

Apologizing is a sign of strength, character, and principles. So don't puss out and put it off. And don't be timid when you do it. It's time to man (or woman) up and make it right.

KEEP IT REAL

Don't mail it in. Or email or text it in for that matter. A badass apology starts face to marker-tagged face.

SPEAK FROM YOUR HEART

This is no time for BS. You need to be genuine and heartfelt. Half-assed or insincere just don't work. Opening yourself only makes you more likeable—which will help the next time you screw up.

OR SPEAK FROM A GOOD SCRIPT

Like this: "I wanted to come and apologize because I really do care about this relationship. I know I hurt you and I am so very sorry for [state your specific misdeed]. I promise [state what you are going to do differently in the future]. I understand you're upset now, and I can only hope that I have a chance to prove myself to you. In the meantime, I'd like to buy you a [insert their favorite drink or 'a copy of *The Book of Party the Animal*']."

Documenting the Party Animal

PART OF THE PARTY ANIMAL'S ALLURE in the social tribe is her ability to create memorable moments—those pieces of cultural capital only increase in value over time and retelling. So the surest way to document these happenings is with appropriate party photography.

ACCEPTABLE PARTY ANIMAL POSES

These are a few of the proven on-camera poses that will best represent the awesomeness.

DEVIL HORNS
Heavy Metal–inspired gestures come and go, but the Devil Horns are here to stay. Adopted by Coven vocalist Jinx Dawson in the late 1960s, and popularized by Ronnie James Dio in the 1980s, this badass symbol has since spread its way across America, popping up everywhere from sporting events to the Miss America Pageant.

THE HUMAN SHELF
Sometimes the best party poses involve a gaggle of your fellow partiers. Take the Human Shelf, for example. This classic pose is executed by having three to five partiers support you as you languidly stretch out in their arms.

THE MIDAIR POSE
Anything captured midair is cool. Jumping off a shed into the pool? Cool. Throwing a keg across the room? Cool. Taking a photo of someone taking a photo of the winning beer pong shot just as it goes in? Meta, but cool.

THE SUPERMAN

Fans often debate about who the greatest superhero of all time is, but there's no debate over which superhero has the greatest pose. It's Superman, by a long shot. You too can emulate the Man of Steel by looking over your right shoulder as you pretend to hold your shirt open at the center.

NOT ACCEPTABLE PARTY ANIMAL POSES

The rise in personal photography has created a rise in unfortunate trends in party poses. Please avoid any of the following party photo fouls:

DUCK LIPS

No one wants to see you pout or purse your lips in your photos. It's an insult to ducks and an even greater insult to humanity.

FLEXING

Do you have 36-inch pythons? Have you ever won a Mr. Olympia competition? If you answered no to either of these questions then you probably shouldn't flex in public.

FAKE GANG SIGNS

Yes, you're a colossal badass. We get it. Until, of course, you run across someone in a real gang with real gang signs. Then you should be ashamed of your fronting. And you might be killed, too.

The Art of Photo Bombing

PHOTO BOMBING IS THE ACT OF HIJACKING A PHOTO, and it's nearly as old as photography itself. Look back far enough and you'll probably even be able to spot some zany Victorian guy making a creepy face in Louis Daguerre's very first metal-plated portrait.

THE CREEPY FACE

A true staple of photobombing, the Creepy Face is best executed by opening your eyelids as wide as possible and staring straight ahead. Think "Charles Manson on a day pass" and you'll be able to nail it every time.

THE PROJECTILE

Recent studies have shown that nine out of ten Americans don't appreciate being puked on. That's why the midair vomit is such a perfect photobombing technique. Simply close your eyes, cover your mouth with both hands, and lurch towards your victims as the photographer snaps their picture.

THE VAN HALEN JUMP

It's impossible not to appreciate the way David Lee Roth would bound all over the stage during the band's heyday. That's why so many photobombers choose to honor "Diamond Dave" by jumping in midair with their arms and legs splayed just as a photo is being snapped.

THE CANNIBAL

Position yourself behind the subject and bring your open, salivating mouth close to their head. If you have been doing bath salts, don't attempt to pretend to bite someone—it might be too tempting.

Do's and Don'ts for Party Games

DO

Have Fun—When drinking's involved, even if you lose you still win.

Always Accept a Challenge—Never back down.

Know the Rules—Don't fall victim to random house rule variations.

Quit While You're Ahead—Just a few games is all you need to prove yourself.

Deal Cards Clockwise—Starting from your left.

DON'T

Be Overcompetitive—It's a party, not the Olympics.

Don't Cheat—Honor and integrity are what a Party Animal should demonstrate.

Don't Hog the Table—Just to reiterate, we're here to party not just play games.

Don't Leave in the Middle—Party Animals don't just peace out, they announce it at least one full game before.

Don't Be a Poor Sport—If you lose, bow out gracefully and get back to partying.

THERE ARE PLENTY OF PARTY GAMES OUT THERE, enough to write a whole other book. (We actually did; it's called *The Book of Beer Awesomeness*—check it out for the complete rules.) A Party Animal must be able to master and dominate every aspect of a party, even the games. And these are the Top Four games necessary to include in your arsenal to form better bonds—and better buzzes.

1. BEER PONG
A.K.A. BEIRUT, PONG

More than a drinking game, it's a drinking sport. Two competitors (or two teams of competitors) throw table tennis balls at formations of plastic cups full of beer.

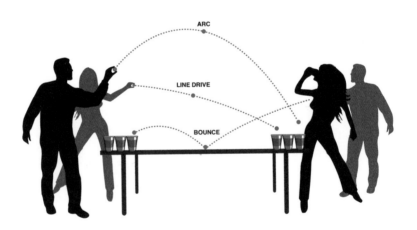

2. FLIP CUP

A.K.A. FLIPPY, FLIPPER, TIPPY CUP

The next in line for a drinking game sensation. Teams stand on opposite sides of a table with cups of beer in front of each player. The first person on each team must chug the beer and then flip the cup over before the next player can go. First team to finish wins.

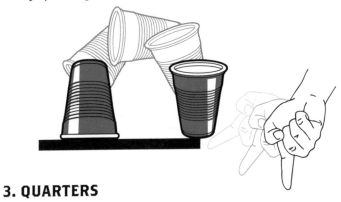

3. QUARTERS

A.K.A. QUATAS, COINAGE, MONEDITA, 25 CENT

A staple at any well-lubricated party, this lively game is believed to have originated in the United States and has since gained popularity in Canada, England, Australia, Germany, and especially South America, where it's better known as Monedita. While the rules may change, the basic premise is the same: Players must bounce a quarter into a cup. It's that simple.

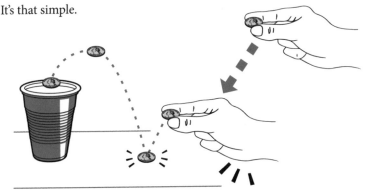

4. ASSHOLE

A.K.A. PRESIDENT, SCHLUB, SCUMBAG

Asshole requires mental dexterity and a degree of cunning. It also relies on our innate need to both subjugate and displace our peers in even the most ramshackle hierarchy. The players compete to be the President (who creates the rules and receives an unfair advantage) and avoid becoming the dreaded Asshole (who does the dealing and gets the beers).

PARTY FOUL

WARNING

PARTY FOUL

EJECTION

CHAPTER
· · **6** · ·

Controlled Chaos

———— ◆ ————

WHEN ANIMALS ATTACK

———— ◆ ————

THERE ARE TIMES WHEN A PARTY ANIMAL HAS NO CHOICE BUT to let their innermost primal instincts take control.

We cannot discourage these acts of disorder—it is what it is, a part of our nature. Can we look down upon a shark for feeding on a smaller fish, or a monkey for flinging its own poo? We think not. Who are we to deny one's true nature?

From pass-out pranks to strategic streaking strategies, this chapter will teach you how to control and channel this inner mayhem and also advise you on how to get away with it and smooth things over when you let your inner monkey out.

It is the Party Animal's role—even right—to help create an atmosphere that is on the verge of utter chaos. It's time to unleash the Beast.

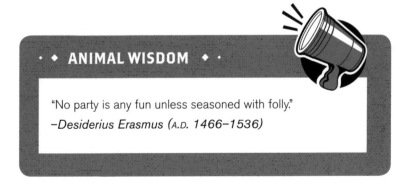

· ◆ ANIMAL WISDOM ◆ ·

"No party is any fun unless seasoned with folly."
–*Desiderius Erasmus* (A.D. *1466–1536)*

Basics of Busting Chops

WHETHER IT'S BALLS OR CHOPS, busting on the rest of the pack is critical to the maintaining of a base level of unpredictability and productive tension. Parties are social affairs. But talking smack doesn't always come easy. Follow this guide, and you'll be the sultan of smackdowns.

MAKE SURE THERE'S A CROWD

You could have the best bust in the world, but what does it matter if nobody is there to laugh at it?

KNOW YOUR ENEMY

The funniest jokes come from the truth. If you know the weaknesses and failures of the chop bustee, you'll have that much more ammo.

KNOW YOURSELF

Just as you'll be sizing up the enemy, so will he be sizing you up. By knowing your own weakness, you won't be as shaken when he attacks them.

COUNTER

Escalation is a natural occurrence in a ball-busting competition. Once your opponent comes back, try knocking him back with something only slightly more powerful. Just remember to always . . .

K.I.S.S.

As in, Keep It Simple, Stupid. By keeping your busts simple and short, they'll remain breezy and fun. The longer, more in-depth a bust is, the more personal it will sound. And when it gets personal, things get nasty.

THE PUNCH GAME

A.K.A. THE CIRCLE GAME, P-NUCKLE

Players: Unlimited

Materials: Two fingers

Gameplay: Players try to trick their opponents into looking directly at the player's hand, which is gesturing an upside-down OK sign. If opponent looks directly at the hand, then player is allowed one punch in the arm. The circle must be below the waist to qualify. If the target is able to break the circle with his finger, then he is able to punch the would-be prankster instead.

THE HUMAN SPRINKLER

A.K.A. SPRAY AND WASH, PISS AND SPIN

Players: At least two dudes

Materials: A urinal and one unsuspecting victim

Gameplay: When your buddy is doing his business at the urinal, grab him by the shoulders mid-flow and start spinning him around. You should be safe from the stream while he is confused and unable to stop the torrent.

BUFFALO CLUB

A.K.A. BUFFALO, THE CLUB

Players: Unlimited

Materials: Hands, and drinks

Gameplay: All initiated players must hold and drink beer in their non-dominant hand at all times. If somebody yells "Buffalo Club!" out loud when you are holding a beer in your dominant hand, you must drink the rest of the beer you're holding. If you call "Buffalo Club!" on somebody when he is actually holding the beer with the proper hand, he may call "False Buffalo!" and you are obligated to finish your own beer.

Pranks

YES, PRANKS ARE FUN AND FUNNY. But they are also critical to the Party Animal's role as the social adhesive for the group—the source of transcendental magnetism. Pranks also play several roles in maintaining these bonds.

THE BENEFITS OF PRANKING

1. Pranks say thanks. The opposite of love is not hate, it's being ignored. So being the target of a prank is a form of attention and appreciation. It's why initiation rituals often involve a good pants-shitting. Nothing says welcome like a bed full of baloney slices.

2. Pranks prevent pricks. Pranks are an acceptable way to keep a pack member's head from getting too big. Recent research suggests that the experience of being duped can stir self-reflection in a way few other experiences can, functioning as a check on arrogance or obliviousness. It levels the playing field for the whole tribe.

3. Pranks create memories. Great pranks create synesthetic experiences, which are unmistakably exciting, original, and reverberating, as well as creative, poetic, and artistic. In other words, they create really memorable events that you'll talk about forever.

PASS-OUT SHAMINGS

The following pranks are designed to mess with a passed-out posse member. They may seem mean-spirited. But they come from a place of love—and revenge.

DUCT TAPE COCOON

Duct tape a drunken, passed out guest inside a tight cocoon to prevent easy movement when they wake up and have to pee. Bonus points if you cocoon them to a tree or wall or even the ceiling.

BOTTLE TRAP

This prank employs two things in plentiful supply at most parties: empty beer bottles and a passed-out victim. Simply place bottles all around the person so when they wake up they won't be able to move without knocking them down. You can be especially evil and use full beer bottles and make cleanup that much more painful.

ANTIQUING

This is not the kind that involves picking through the knickknacks on a Saturday morning; it's taking a handful of flour and throwing it in somebody's face while they are passed out or sleeping (preferably with a hangover).

HUMAN JENGA®

Jenga® is a classic game in which players must stack wooden blocks on a table until one player knocks it over. Now imagine instead of a table it's a passed-out person and instead of wooden blocks it's a yard sale of crap from around the house. Same rules apply.

SHARPIE® SHAMING

A victim of a shaming can often shake it off, take a shower, and move on with only a bruised ego and a hung-over stomach. Unless that is, someone decides to use everyone's favorite indelible marker for a permanent punking.

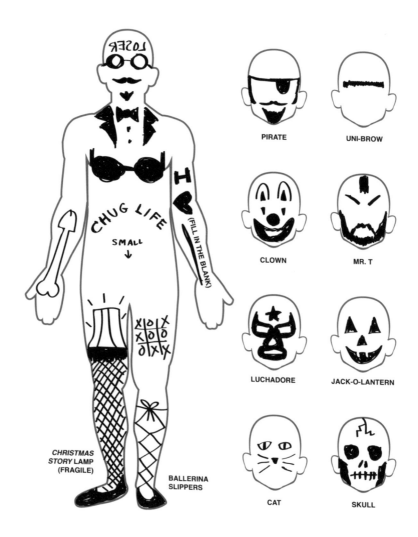

THE BOOK OF THE PARTY ANIMAL

MINOR MISCHIEF

These prankings require a bit more pre-meditation and a bit more cojones to cause a bit more lasting damage.

BLOOD SHOWER

Remove your target's showerhead and place a red Easter egg dye tablet inside. Replace the head and wait for hilarity to ensue. The tablet will dissolve slowly—giving the perfect amount of time for your target to step into the shower before starring in their version of *Carrie.*

SUPER SOAKER SINK

Cause minor mayhem with just one rubber band. Place it around the trigger on the hand-sprayer on a kitchen sink. Anytime someone turns on water they will be greeted with a surprise stream up in their business.

REVERSE BATHROOM

It's not uncommon for some party hosts to use the bathtub as a giant beer cooler. To mess with guests, simply take the cold beer and ice out of the tub and put it in the toilet bowl tank and the sink. Not only will this make people think twice about reaching for a beer, but it will also force them to use the bathtub as a toilet. That'll teach the host not to cheap out on a proper cooler.

PRANKING VS. BULLYING ETIQUETTE

If there is one thing a Party Animal is not, it's a bully. There is a big line between Pranking and Bullying and that line should never be crossed. Pranking is a friendly, light-hearted banter between friends that results in "ooohs and aaahs" rather than tears and blood.

According to StopBullying.gov, bullying is defined as "un-wanted, aggressive behavior that involves a real or perceived power imbalance. Bullying includes actions such as making threats, spreading rumors, attacking someone physically or verbally, and excluding someone from a group on purpose."

Pretty clear, right? So just don't do those things and have some fun breaking some balls.

Other Pranks with Duct Tape

- **THE SILVER BAND-AID**–Place the duct tape on the victim's hairiest body parts. Then, enjoy a morning full of screams of agony and confusion when they attempt to pull off the tape.

- **DUCT DRAWERS**–Like the Cocoon, but focused on the midsection only. Create a pair of bulletproof boxers and watch them try to get out before nature runs its course.

- **DUCT DOORWAY**–On the outer side of the victim's door, start taping long strips across the doorframe. When they wake up and stumble outside of their room they'll be confused and, with any luck, stick to this human-size flypaper.

Top Human Jenga Moves

- Cigarette in mouth
- Cup balanced on head
- Bucket on head
- Bananas in suggestive positions
- Bra on head
- Couch cushions
- Compliant pets

Top Sharpie Shamings

- Evil villain moustache
- Penis on forehead
- Goatee
- "Loser"
- Hitler moustache
- Eye Patch
- A combination of all of the above

LESS MINOR MISCHIEF

Applying the following pranks will allow a skilled Party Animal
to create more havoc and a few more enemies.

FANNINGS

The ceiling fan, an often overlooked appliance that can be the perfect
muse for mischief. One simple usage is to secretly place foreign objects
onto the top of the fan's paddles. These objects will remain virtually
invisible until the victim turns it on—at which time it will scatter the
payload around the room. Here are some suggestions.

Pennies · These will be pennies from hell when they begin flying
around the room.

Kool-Aid® · The flavored sugar makes a great drink but an even better
prank to clean out of everything.

Glitter · Make their room look like a fairy murder scene with copious
handfuls flying around.

DOOR TSUNAMI

This prank is best played on someone in a dorm or hotel—any place you
are not responsible for any kind of structural integrity. When the target
is in her room, fill a trash can three-quarters full of cold water. (Freezing
cold water will also do.) Lean the trash can against her door and knock.
The rest will take care of itself.

TOP SHELVING

Also known as Upper Decking, this is a prank that keeps on giving—
long after it is pulled off. The first step is to get some quality time with
your target's toilet. Remove the lid from the reservoir and perch your
hindquarters over the upper bowl. Release the hounds—in other words,
poop. Then place the lid back on. The result will be a stink from the
bathroom that only gets worse the more they flush it.

PEESICLE

This prank takes some preparation, an empty freezer, a metal tray, and a devious mind. The recipe, however, is simple: Collect some urine and pour it onto the tray. Place in freezer until, you guessed it, frozen. Then, pull the frozen pee-plane off and slide it under the target's door. With any luck they will awake to find a puddle of pee in the middle of their locked room.

Destruction

SOMETIMES YOU NEED TO TAKE THE CHAOS TO 11. And by 11 we mean breaking stuff like a madman with 'roid rage.

TRASHING A HOTEL ROOM LIKE A ROCK STAR

A hotel room is the perfect canvas for Party Animals to exercise their chaotic creativity—and upper body as we'll soon find out. But realizing the art of the drunken possibility doesn't happen after leaving a few towels on the floor or booting in the bathroom sink.

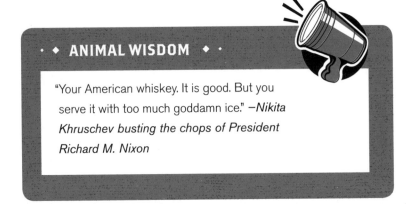

◆ ANIMAL WISDOM ◆ ◆

"Your American whiskey. It is good. But you serve it with too much goddamn ice." —*Nikita Khruschev busting the chops of President Richard M. Nixon*

No, a true Party Animal must stand on the shoulders of giants—then jump off those shoulders and trash the shit out of the Sheraton®. So here are four proven moves perfected by the gods of rock.

THE AMY WINEHOUSE

Chuck your dinner against the wall. The late Amy Winehouse infamously hurled a plate of spaghetti Bolognese across the room of a hotel. This a good choice since the high viscosity of sauce will help distribute but not dissipate the mess over the area. In addition, the red tomatoes will contrast with the stains and provide a certain inside-the-car-in-*Pulp Fiction* atmosphere.

Acceptable and Unacceptable Things to Destroy

ACCEPTABLE	UNACCEPTABLE
Plastic Party Cups	Glassware
Empties	Full Bottles
Photos of Your Ex	Family Photos
Tube TVs	LED TVs
Your Own Furniture	Someone Else's Furniture
Your To-Do List	The Beer Pong Table List
Burnt-Out Light Bulbs	CFL Bulbs (they're hazardous)

THE KEITH MOON

The late Who's drummer provided a multi-textured trash on his infamous twenty-first birthday in 1967. He toppled a five-tier cake to start a food fight, discharged all of the fire extinguishers in the hallway, and dropped someone's Lincoln Continental™ into the Holiday Inn®'s pool. That is how to trash a hotel.

THE KEITH RICHARDS

At the L.A. stop of the Rolling Stones' 1972 North American tour, the immortal Keith Richards created the ultimate sign of rock-star destruction by hurling a TV off the balcony on the tenth floor. The most amazing thing is to imagine Keith's frail frame holding a pre–flat screen TV set. But if he can do it, you can certainly can too.

THE AEROSMITH

This band of old professional trashers actually traveled with props so they could properly get the trashing job done—chainsaws for furniture and extension cords for throwing TVs out the window. So the moral of this story is, come prepared to bring it!

If sitcoms have taught us anything, it is that a pregnant woman will always go into labor when stuck in an elevator. And that and out-of-control house parties will always result in the slow-motion breaking of an expensive vase. Party Animals will always be held responsible for this, so it's important to know how to rectify it.

1. SURVEY THE DAMAGE

If it's only a simple chip or crack, you can use some ceramic cement as directed in the next step. If it's worse, you'll need to proceed to step 3—and have much more patience.

2. EASY PIECES

If it's a whole chip that fits back into the area, take a deep breath and know it's going to be okay. Use some sandpaper to lightly clean the edges of the piece and its location on the vase. Use some ceramic cement and hold for least two minutes—then let dry for three hours. Use a razor blade to trim off excess glue. Wipe your brow and don't tell a soul.

3. MORE EXTREME MEASURES

If after replacing the pieces with the technique above there is a still a missing chunk, you'll need to roll up your sleeves and roll out some wall putty. Use masking tape to secure the back of the surrounding area, then use the straight side of a butter knife to spread the putty to fill the area. Let it dry overnight and try to match the paint color. A clear sealant will give it the shine and texture of the original ceramic.

4. FAKE ITS DEATH

If it's not looking anything like new, then you'll need to go to next level of deception. Place the vase back in its original location, with the least damaged side facing out. Then stage a welcome back "surprise" party—complete with banner and streamers. When the hosts return, jump out to say "Welcome Back!" and "accidently" knock off the vase with the giant bouquet of flowers you were about to present them with. Who could be mad at that?

TOSSING A KEG LIKE A PRO

Oftentimes, destruction takes place as an unintended consequence of running out of booze. But just because the keg is tapped doesn't mean the party's over. The keg toss keeps the party going and testosterone flowing.

HEIGHT

To emulate your favorite strongman competition, use the pendulum method. From the pre-NBA free-throw stance, use a fluid (no pun intended) swinging motion with the keg between your legs to generate some momentum. Release backward over your head at the apex of your swing.

DISTANCE

This is an ode to Thor. Like throwing a mighty hammer, discus, or little person, the key is centrifugal force. Hold the top of the keg with both hands and begin moving your whole body in a circular spinning movement. Increase the speed, picking up momentum and extreme dizziness until you release the keg in the general direction you want.

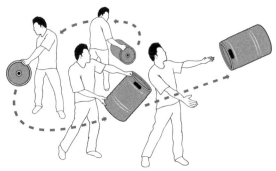

Clip-'n'-Save Release Form

Sometimes debauchery and destruction are par for the course.
Protect yourself with this handy agreement.

LIABILITY RELEASE FORM

On this _____ day of _____, 20___, intending
     DATE   MONTH   YEAR

to be legally bound hereby, the undersigned Party Host agrees

and does hereby release from liability and to indemnify and hold

harmless _____, in regards to the Party
                    YOUR NAME

and Events located at _____. This release
                           LOCATION OF PARTY

is for any and all liability for personal injuries and property losses

or damage occasioned by, or in connection with any activity

performed at this event.

_____   _____
PARTY HOST'S SIGNATURE   YOUR SIGNATURE

_____   _____
PARTY HOST'S PRINTED NAME   YOUR PRINTED NAME

The Naked Animal

THOUGH PARTY ANIMALS ARE KNOWN TO BE quite fashionable, it should be noted that clothes do not always make the man (or woman). In fact, for a Party Animal to truly embrace the more primal nature of his endeavors, it's only fitting that he shed his clothes to better resemble the animal he behaves like. In other words, like the Shakespearean sonnet goes: It ain't a party 'til someone gets nekked.

NUDITY STRATEGIES

While the naked body is a natural part of life, the Party Animal is able to see it as more: It is an opportunity to take the party, which is here [making a low motion with hands] to that which will be here [moving hands over head]. Like the naked body itself, no two reasons for getting naked are alike. But here are the general themes:

Party catalyst • When it's time to get the party started and rally the crowd, a nude partier signals to everyone that it's on like Donkey Kong.

Courting • Being a sexual beast, the Party Animal also uses the strategic nudity as a way of displaying the hardware (or software) to potential buyers.

• ◆ ANIMAL WISDOM ◆ •

"You moon the wrong person at an office party and suddenly you're not 'professional' any more."—*Jeff Foxworthy*

Protest · In a few instances, as we will see with mooning, nudity can be used for cultural provocation.

NUDITY TECHNIQUES

MOONING

This classic ass exposure dates back to at least the 1300s, when French soldiers flashed their derrieres to the British archers. With over 700 years of further evolution, mooning has become more than a flash in the pan, but the de facto way to both expose yourself and deflate your opponents. Below are some of the most memorable moons.

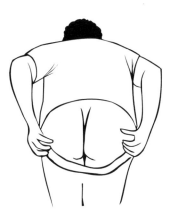

Full Moon · With feet planted about a shoulder-width apart, the mooner bends at the waist and the knees while pulling down their pants to expose their bare hindquarters.

Flashing a Brown Eye · A full moon but with the addition of a manual spreading of the cheeks.

Pressed Ham · A full moon that is pressed against a glass window. Often done from a car, but said ham can be pressed against any glass to impress spectators.

Growler · Also known as a Full Moon with Stick Out, a Red-Eyed Rooster, or simply a Fruit Salad, this is a full moon with male genitals tucked under and exposed.

Moon Man • This a moon in which the mooner has drawn a face on his or her buttocks. By placing a pair of sunglasses on the moon face, it is called a Tom Cruise Moon.

FLASHING

Mooning always involves just the backside, and is predominantly done for protest and jest. Here are several other famous flashing techniques to apply to your party.

The Mardi Gras Flash • This is the classic act of girls going wild. It involves an exposure of one's breasts to get someone to throw beads or throw them off their beer pong game.

The Jerry Springer Flash • A newer form of female breast flashing, this is done as an insult and is often performed by someone whom you would not want to see exposed.

The Dinner Roll Flash • In this act, a male lets his "beans" hang out of his fly and nonchalantly goes about his business. He allows others to take an unfortunate glance down, at which point he asks the victim, "Care for a dinner roll?" It's quite classy.

The Meat Spin Flash • A male Party Animal can incite a crowd by performing this brazen act of exposure. It's a full body flash with the addition of a fanlike action caused by the rhythmic rotation of one's hips and, well, wiener.

PARTIAL NUDITY STUNTS

Not everyone has the balls to go full nude. So here are several
adult alternatives:

Assless Chapping · Chaps tell the world you know your way around a
horse. Assless chaps tell the world you know your way around the party.

Body Shots · While the exposure level is conservative, body shots are
one of the few tactics that invite contact. In one version, a person lays
on the bar holding a lime in her mouth and dabs salt on a body part.
The shooter licks the salt, takes shot of tequila, and sucks the lime from
the other person's mouth. Another version has the shot actually poured
into the bellybutton of the prone participant.

Porky Pig-ing · Taking a clue from everyone's favorite stuttering
pig, this is the combination of class and crass. The setup is simple—
formalwear on top, bare ass on the bottom.

Tube Socking · Inspired by the Red Hot Chili Peppers, this is a great
way to finally use all those single socks. The male flasher places his junk
in the tube sock and does his best elephant impression.

> · ◆ **PARTY FACT** ◆ ·
>
> Originating in Orange County, California, the
> Annual Mooning of Amtrak is a long-running tradition
> in which people spend the greater part of the day—
> risking sunburn to their parts—to moon the passenger
> trains as they roll by.

COMPETITIVE NUDITY

Some nudity is just for fun. Some nudity is for games. The following activities combine exposure with competition for a wild mix.

Wet T-shirt Contest • This is the universal symbol of the American spring break experience. And now with the proliferation of cellphone cameras, your school, parents, and one day, grandkids, will be able to see your experience as well.

Naked Chicken • Like a Roman gladiator match, but instead of wielding weapons the two competitors see who will take off the most clothes. Two people enter, one leaves nekkid.

Strip Poker • Another classic Party Animal staple. And while some things never change, the extreme popularity of poker has led to some strip poker professionals keeping their wrap-around glasses on—even in the buff.

Strip Pong • Beer Pong, the sport of champions, has also spawned a nude-friendly version of the game. Words for articles of clothes are written on the bottom of the cups. When a ball lands in that cup, one of the team members must remove that article—and drink the beer.

Naked Fundraiser • Taking a cue from the movie *Major League*, a good-looking person donates his or her body to the greater good. They accept donations to remove a piece of clothing for a set price— money goes to charity, the party fund, or their own pocket. If the party combines to offer one big sum and the contestant accepts, he/she stays naked all night.

How to Streak like You Mean It

By Chris Barish, Author of *The Book of Bad*

Getting naked and running around is one thing. But streaking is a discrete skill. The Party Animal knows that pulling it off takes more than just taking it off. Here are some tips for streaking like a pro:

PLACE UNDERWEAR ON HEAD

More than just a chic hat, it gives you a quick escape option so that a cop doesn't hit you with an indecent exposure charge.

WEAR SHOES

Remember, you're running. Shows onlookers that you know your shit. And it allows you to avoid would-be captors with ease.

PROTECT YOUR GOODS

Perhaps you are celebrating the first snowfall of the year. Be mindful of ill-advised frostbite and consider wearing a glove or sock as a precaution. And in the blazing summer sun it's recommended you apply sunblock (or have someone special apply it for you).

PLAN THE GETAWAY

Plan your route in advance like a pro. Have your friends waiting in a car to whisk you away. All that's left behind is your impressive description and Party Animal scent.

A RECENT STUDY BY THE PARTY ANIMAL INSTITUTE OF AMERICA (PAIA) found that Party Animals mate nearly five times as frequently as regular civilians. Although the finding isn't terribly surprising, the study did break new ground by pinpointing the top reasons why Party Animals do the "featherbed jig" so often.

1. Attraction of the Alpha • Like all Alphas, Party Animals assert their dominance in social situations. And as National Geographic has taught us, the Alpha oozes with attraction to the rest of the tribe.

2. The Power of the Provider • In addition to the seduction of social status, individuals can't help but be lured by the pull of someone who can provide. With the Party Animal's ability to produce Jell-O® shots, pizza, and various party paraphernalia out of thin night air, it is no wonder they are regarded for their ability to take care of the tribe.

3. Blame it on the A-A-Adrenaline. • Research shows that when individuals experience surges of adrenaline together they are more likely to have feelings of attraction for each other. Adrenaline is the substance of choice for a Party Animal. So after being chased by the cops, crashing a wedding, and road tripping to Vegas, prospective mates are virtually blinded with biological lust.

THE MATING ANIMAL

A Party Animal is a little bit like hydrogen: He's relatively harmless on his own, but he can be incredibly destructive when combined with the wrong element. That's why it's crucial to ensure he chooses the right mate. Following are three types of potential mates, with a cautionary note for each.

How to Talk to a Cop

America's police officers are a critical part of keeping our society open for Party Animals like you to have the freedom to party. But sometimes the forces of police and the forces of party intersect. Here are some easy points about dealing with the po-po:

1. KEEP CALM AND CARRY ON

Don't freak out. The cops don't know what is around each corner, so they will be rightfully suspicious about what's going down. So stay cool. Don't try to make a dash or speed away.

2. DON'T TALK BACK

This is no time to flex your knowledge of the legal system from watching DVDs of *Law & Order*. It's no time to talk about oppression, or the system, or the man.

3. DON'T TALK MUCH AT ALL

Whether you are guilty or innocent, you don't need to answer anything other than your name (and possibly your address). Anything else is consent. If the cop asks, "Can I talk to you?" say something like "I'm sorry, I'm in a hurry and I don't have time to talk to you right now." If the cop insists, ask him, "Am I free to leave?" If he says, "Yes," then walk the f** away.

4. IF WORSE COMES TO WORSE, STILL DON'T TALK

Even if for whatever reason, you do get arrested, don't resist. Don't argue. But don't start yapping either. The magic phrase is: "I am going to remain silent. I want to see a lawyer." Just keep repeating it.

Party Animal Pick-Up Lines

Knowing what to say to a member of the opposite sex isn't easy, even for a Party Animal. That's why it's always a good idea to have a few humorous pick-up lines at your disposal for those occasions when you find yourself tongue-tied.

"Can I buy you a drink, or do you just want the money?"

"Excuse me, do you have your phone number? I seem to have lost mine."

"I'm new in town. Could I have directions to your place?"

"I'm not actually this tall. I'm sitting on my wallet."

"Can I buy you a drink so I look better?"

"Inheriting eighty million bucks doesn't mean much when you have a weak heart."

"Do you believe in love at first sight? Because I can walk by again."

"Bedtime already?"

"Hi. I suffer from amnesia. Do I come here often?"

"Shall we talk or continue flirting from a distance?"

"So, what do you like for breakfast?"

"So, what haven't you been told tonight?"

"Blink if you're interested in me."

"Excuse me, but did you happen to find my Congressional Medal of Honor?"

WALLFLOWERS

Austrian psychoanalyst Theodore Reik first asserted that opposites attract. Or maybe it was Paula Abdul. Either way, humans often choose partners who possess the qualities we feel we're lacking. That's why painfully shy Wallflowers often gravitate towards Party Animals. Sadly, this partnership is doomed to fail since the Party Animal's extroverted personality brings the Wallflower into too many foreign and uncomfortable situations.

OTHER PARTY ANIMALS

Imagine a lion mating with a shark. That's akin to what happens when two Party Animals decide to shack up. Whether it's for one night, one hour, or one minute, their union almost always results in a crazy, tumultuous hurricane of unbridled passion. It's loud, it's heated, it's intense, and like most hurricanes, it usually ends with someone's house being torn to shreds.

THE MATE OF ANOTHER PARTY ANIMAL

This is some serious Jane Goodall–type stuff. The ensuing tussling of two tribes usually results in at least one person spending the night in the clink. And for what? Another Party Animal's sloppy seconds. This is one leftover dish that's best left untouched.

HOW TO INCREASE YOUR ANIMAL MAGNETISM

SHOW SOME SCENT SENSIBILITY

Our bodies produce powerful pheromones that are undetectable to the human nose. Pheromones are airborne secretions that relay important information and can trigger a sexual response. Thanks to new advances in science, you can now enhance your desirability by using pheromone cologne. While their claims are questionable, they at least do a commendable job of masking your personal funk.

DEMONSTRATE SUPREME CONFIDENCE

Green Bay Packers coach Vince Lombardi once said, "Confidence is contagious. So is lack of confidence." So stand tall, make eye contact, smile, don't fidget, and always speak with conviction. In other words, do everything your mother told you to do when you were seven.

SHOW YOUR THING

No, we're not suggesting you should flash your goods—at least not at the beginning of the evening. You should, however, show off your one special skill that you do better than anyone else. If you can sing, jump on stage. If you can draw, do a doodle. If you can juggle . . . well keep that to yourself and try to sing instead. Mates love to see mastery, and your talent could help seal the deal.

DANCE

It's been said that dancing is just a vertical expression of a horizontal desire. By showing off your moves on the floor you're signaling that you also have moves in the bedroom . . . and under the bleachers . . . and in the backseat of your car . . . and in the supply closet in your office . . .

MATING LOCATIONS

A Party Animal can't always control when and where he'll be when he finds a willing partner. Here are five locations for your next impromptu romantic encounter:

ON TOP OF THE WASHING MACHINE

There's a fine line between coming clean and getting dirty, especially when you're laying pipe on top of a washing machine.
PRO: The machine's powerful vibrations are sure to spice things up.
CON: Your behavior might get you kicked out of the laundromat.

IN A CLOSET

Closets are no longer just for mops and cleaning supplies, especially when a horny Party Animal is on the loose.

PRO: The pitch darkness allows you and your partner to fantasize that you're making love to someone far more attractive.

CON: Having to stand up severely limits the number of positions you can try.

ON THE KITCHEN TABLE

We all know things can really heat up in the kitchen, particularly when a Party Animal's libido starts boiling over.

PRO: The proximity to the fridge allows you to get creative with lots of tasty props.

CON: The rest of the people at the table may not appreciate your grunting and groaning as they try to enjoy their meal.

IN A BATHROOM

If your definition of safe sex is locking the door first, then a bathroom is definitely the place for you.

PRO: Bathrooms provide an unmatched level of privacy and comfort.

CON: You may get mobbed by an angry horde of partiers who have been waiting to use the toilet.

IN A PARKED CAR

You can tell a lot about a Party Animal from his car—particularly if you count the number of different shoe impressions on his windshield.

PRO: You can park in any number of romantic locations. Or in front of a dumpster. The choice is up to you!

CON: If you're not careful, you can get buggered by your stick shift.

CHAPTER

· · **7** · ·

Call of the Wild

·

COMMUNICATION

PARTY ANIMALS ARE QUITE POSSIBLY THE MOST SOCIAL CREATURES on the face of the planet—and occasionally its backside too. This means that they are also master communicators.

As we've seen, they have the ability to inspire people to take action—or inspire people to be in awe as they thrust on the dance floor. They can uplift people to great heights of the night—or take the piss out of someone and bring them back to earth.

The best way to truly understand the Party Animal's amazing gift for communication is to parse out their parlance—understanding their words, phrases and grunts.

So what follows is a survey of the lingua franca of this species—the lexical landscape. Some of these terms will be self-evident. Some might even sound foreign. Or worse, French. Regardless of the pronunciation, this should provide you a glimpse into the language of raging.

> **· ◆ ANIMAL WISDOM ◆ ·**
>
> "Hear no evil, speak no evil—and you'll never be invited to a party."*–Oscar Wilde*

· *Rally Cries* ·

SOMETIMES WORDS JUST AREN'T ENOUGH, but, then again, sometimes they're just too much. Enter the guttural, primitive rally cry. It's a preverbal expression that Party Animals and their packs are pre-programmed to respond to.

Rally cries predate language. Anthropologists suggest that early hominids would use these calls to signal attacks and announce feasts. In both cases it's a sign of bonding—as the individuals of the group organize as one to fight and feed.

There are many ways to pump up a crowd, but none of them is as instantaneous as a good old-fashioned rally cry. Long, loud, and impossible to ignore, these throaty call to arms get a crowd's attention and awaken a primal instinct to wreak havoc. Rally cries are perfect for:

- *Jetting* a party started
- *Resuscitating* a flagging party
- *Leading* a panty raid
- *Convincing* your fellow partiers to streak
- *Inspiring* someone to take a drink
- *Jetting* a hot chick to show you her sweater kittens
- *Kicking* off a keg stand

Examine the following catalog of cries to determine which "Call of the Wild" is calling your name.

"GERONIMO!"

Few warriors have ever possessed more courage than Geronimo, an Apache chief who bravely defended his homeland against a wave of colonization during the late nineteenth century. His daring deeds made his name synonymous with fearlessness and prompted U.S. paratroopers to begin shouting it out prior to jumping out of their planes.

"HOOAH"

No one knows the origin of this ubiquitous battle cry, but U.S. soldiers have been using it since World War II as an expression of high morale, fortitude, and confidence. "Hooah" has also been known to mean other things such as:

* Roger
* Yes, sir
* Thank you
* You just discharged your rifle in my foot

"OH YEEAHH!"

Anyone who grew up in the 1980s knew there was a strong possibility that a six-foot-tall pitcher of cherry Kool-Aid® would come bursting through your wall whenever you casually mentioned you were thirsty. And when he did, the larger-than-life Kool-Aid® Man would

HISTORIC RALLY CRIES

As you develop your own rally cry, consider borrowing some inspiration from these historically significant screams.

"Alala!"

Greek warriors would scream this war cry in tribute to Athena, the goddess of war.

"Euoi"

Ancient Greeks would also holler this during the orgies of the Bacchanalia festivals.

"Ay-bas!"

Turkic tribes screamed this call to the power of the moon during the Middle Ages.

"Woh-who-ey!"

This is the actual Rebel Yell used by Confederate soldiers during the Civil War.

invariably bellow out "Oh, yeeahh!" You didn't question it, you were just grateful to have a drink that contained enough sugar to sink a battleship.

"OH YEAH!"

On the surface, it's easy to confuse the Kool-Aid® Man's "Oh yeeahh" with Randy "The Macho Man" Savage's "Oh yeah," but any Party Animal will tell you the two are quite different. For starters, the Macho Man's rally cry is short and succinct, while the Kool-Aid® Man draws out his "yeeahh" for a prolonged period of time. Secondly, the Kool-Aid® Man uses his rally cry exclusively as an exclamation, while the Macho Man's "Oh yeah" is also frequently used as an interjection.

"WHOOT WHOOT!"

From 1989 to 1994, it was nearly impossible to mention Arsenio Hall's name without some dork pumping his fist and shouting "Whoot Whoot" at the top of his lungs. And by "dork" we mean "Arsenio Hall." The former talk show host used his signature rally cry multiple times per episode to warm up the crowd, welcome guests, and wake up his band.

"COWABUNGA!"

Often heard by those either a) leading surfers into the waves or b) leading mutant, reptilian ninjas into battle. Either way, this battle cry became almost synonymous with beach parties and rowdy good times.

"WHOOP WHOOP!"

If you hear this call you are in the presence of an entirely different animal species: the Juggalo. These are the fans of the rock-rap group Insane Clown Posse. If you hear it, run for cover to a safe place where they won't find you—like in a library or museum.

"WOOOO!"

This guttural roar is the Esperanto of millennial crowds. From college campuses to concert crowds to stadiums of fans, the extended "Wooo," often accompanied with fist waving, is a sure sign something is about to go down.

"YESSSSSSSSSS!"

Much has been written about Marv Albert's ferret-like hairpiece and proclivity for wearing women's lingerie, but you have to give this veteran jock sniffer props for coming up with one of the greatest rally cries in televised sports. Short, simple, and easily replicated, his distinctive "Yesssssssss!" is the perfect punctuation for any celebratory moment.

"YIKA YIKA YOW!"

Nothing gets a crowd's attention more effectively than a well-timed "Yika Yika Yow!" Just ask Steven Tyler. The androgynous Aerosmith frontman has been using the rally cry for more than forty years to a) get crowds on their feet and b) scream at Joe Perry for stealing his hairspray.

SPEAKING FLUENT PARTY ANIMAL IS EASY. Just memorize the following list of 112 terms and you're good to go.

AIDS (After Intense Drinking Shits) • The post-party impact on the G.I. tract.

Antiqued • When someone passes out or falls asleep early, you coat them with handfuls of flour to make them look old and dusty. *See page 173.*

Ape Shit • To lose control for any number of reasons. "When he found out someone peed on his bed, Barry went ape shit and trashed the bunk beds and dressers."

Around the World • A party theme in which participants move from room to room. Each room is decorated in a theme of a different country and with the appropriate alcoholic beverages provided. *See page 102.*

B.B.D. (Bigger Better Deal) • This is a code word for a Party Animal to let his entourage know they should move on to a better party.

B.O.D. (Breath of Dog) • The hideous breath that one generally has after a long night of beer chuggin', boot knockin', and ganja smokin'. "Shit, dude, I woke up this morning with some killer B.O.D.!"

Bad Idea Jeans • When one behaves in a most idiotic fashion (from a *Saturday Night Live* skit). "The guy trying to touch that cop's gun is wearing Bad Idea Jeans."

Bar Scars • All the wristbands and ink left over after making the rounds at the bars. "By the look of those bar scars, you must have had a good night."

Barbara • Someone who talks incessantly while holding the joint, inhibiting others from smoking (derived from Barbara Walters).

Batten the Hatches • The act of locking the door and placing a towel under it before toking in your dorm room.

Bayonetting the Wounded • Drinking all of the leftover half-full drinks while cleaning up the morning after a party.

Beer Bitch • The person sitting closest to the cooler or refrigerator at a party whose job it is to grab another beer when yours runs out. The most important person in drinking games, especially for the President and the Asshole. *See page 166.*

Beer Dash • Act performed by cheap or broke students who will wait outside a convenience store at night until the clerk is busy, then enter, grab a 6- or 12-pack of beer, and take off running out the door. *A.k.a. Beer Run, Beer Sprint*

Beer Fairy • An undesirable party-goer who provides free alcohol in an attempt to gain friends.

Beer Gnomes • The reason for the random bruises, pains, and lacerations you unexplainably have after a night of heavy drinking.

Beer Goggles • One's perception when under the influence of alcohol. Often causes unattractive people to look hot, long distances to look jumpable, and breakdancing moves to look easy.

Beer Muscles • A sudden increase in courage and combative abilities directly linked to alcohol consumption.

Beer Scooter • After a night on the piss, the ability to walk home five or six miles without noticing the distance, or waking up in your bed without any idea of how you got there. "How did you get home last night?" "Who knows, I must have ridden the beer scooter."

Beeracle • A miracle that is caused by almighty beer. For example, someone making ten straight cups in a game of Beer Pong. *See page 164.*

Beeramid • The ritual of stacking empties in a triangle formation.

Boot and Rally • To drink until you puke, then keep drinking afterwards.

Booze Hound • Someone who drinks in excessive quantities and does so with regularity.

Booze Snooze • A nap taken early in the afternoon to prepare for the night's party, after you've already been drinking.

Breaking the Seal • Going pee-pee for the first time during the night. Once the seal is broken, restroom trips become much more frequent. Usually, followed by an I.S.P. (Inevitable Second Piss) *A.k.a. F.F.P. (Fatal First Pee).*

Breakout • The act of becoming quite intoxicated, then leaving a party without telling anyone. People at the party only notice a few minutes later (depending on your popularity).

B.U.I. (Biking Under the Influence) • When you get drunk and try to ride a bike. "Careful, you don't wanna get a BUI tonight."

Bullet Time • Used to describe the drunken sixth sense you sometimes get at parties that allows you to dodge ex-girlfriends, spilled beer, vomit, etc.

Camping • When someone is talking or spacing out and not passing anyone the marijuana that's in his hands, he's camping with the bowl.

Cashed • Synonym for "stoned"; also used to describe when all the weed in a bowl/pipe/bong has been smoked. "It's cashed, yo—pack another one."

Closing the Borders • When a group denies that they're drinking/smoking in order to keep moochers away.

Collegesque • Being very collegiate at what you do (e.g., boozin', drugs, and sleeping around).

Dead Soldier • Empty beer can/bottle.

Deed • To be very, very high from potent marijuana, such as sinsemilla or Hydro. Gaining the term from DE-fense in sports, because you are so high it feels like the dope is on offense and your mind is playing defense. *A.k.a. D'ed.*

D.O.A. (Drunk on Arrival) • Getting drunk before going to a party, club, or class. "This party might be good, but I think we should be DOA just to be safe."

Double-Fisting • The art and science of holding and consuming two drinks at once.

Drunken Black Hole • The cosmic force that delivers you to your room even though you have no idea how you got there.

Drunkenese • The language commonly used by incoherent drunks unable to continue speaking English.

D.U.I. (Dialing Under the Influence) • Includes prank calling, booty calls, and other contact with ex–significant others.

English, to be • To drink in a dainty, high society fashion. Drinking just the minimum amount to stay in a club / party.

Fix Stuff • To break stuff. A sometimes alcohol- or sexual-frustration-fuelled rage common in males at 2:00 A.M. often involving bottle breaking and chest pounding.

Flagged ◆ To be cut off from further alcohol consumption following a particularly drunken act. "Jen is flagged; she just spilled her beer on me."

Float a Keg ◆ To finish all the beer, thus making the keg float in its icy bath.

Fratastic ◆ An adjective describing an individual or object that is thoroughly and completely steeped in fraternity life.

Fruit Salad ◆ The act of mooning someone with your testicles tucked between your legs, thus making your scrotum visible to the moon's recipient. In theory, it resembles a bowl of grapes or plums.

Fuzz ◆ Police.
A.k.a. Narc, Po-Po, Pig.

G.D.A. (God Damn Animal) ◆ Synonym for Party Animal.

Go Cup ◆ The cups you get to pour your bottle of beer in when leaving a bar, also used to describe personally made beverages that come with you to whatever festivities you're headed to.

Gong Show ◆ A drunken night.

Grenade ◆ Derived from when you're cleaning up the day after a party and go to grab a beer can you assumed was empty but, being half-full, it falls to the floor and explodes foul-smelling, stale beer/cigarette-butt juice all over the place.
A.k.a. Wounded Soldier.

H.V.T. (High vs. Time) ◆ This is a graph of the effects of a substance on the user as time passes. "Dude, I'm waaaaaaay up on the HVT graph!"

Handle ◆ A 1.5-liter bottle of hard liquor. Named after the handle often crafted into the bottle.
A.k.a. Home Wrecker.

Heel-Toe Express ◆ The only way that poor college kids can get around after public transportation shuts down at 1 A.M.

Hit • When you look so bad after a night of hard drinking/partying that everyone else knows you're still hung over. "You look HIT!"

Hoover • When a beer is spilled, the spiller must drink the beer from whatever surface it is on—regardless of any sanitation concerns.

Hotboxing • Smoking lots of pot in a small contained area, such as a car or single dorm room, making the air so smoky that you are, in effect, taking a hit every time you breathe. *A.k.a. Clambaking, Fishbowling, Greenhousing.*

House Cups • At a party, these are cups of the hosts, which allow them to cut in the keg line and get dibs on the last of the booze.

In the Oven • Metaphor for being extremely stoned.

Jamaican Bobsled Team • Usually three or more people who either a) spend the party on the couch, at the bar, or wherever in a straight or semi-straight line, or b) wait in the line for a hit off a bowl.

Kegs and Eggs • Morning keg party usually before a football game.

Liquid Courage • The fact that you will do things while drunk that you will not do while sober. May lead to the flexing of one's Beer Muscles.

Lockdown • Putting a towel under the door, turning off main lights, leaving only Christmas lights and the lava lamp on. Not answering the door for anyone— open the window, lower the blinds, and toke up. *See Batten the Hatches.*

Locusts • The term used for large groups of freshmen who wander the streets looking for parties. When they find a party they usually drink all the booze, use up all of its resources, and move on to the next.

M.D.A. (Mysterious Drinking Accident) • What happens when you get drunk and hurt yourself in

some way, but don't remember it. Evidence of MDAs includes cuts and bruises and no memory of how you got them.
A.k.a. R.P.I., Random Party Injury; U.B.I., Unidentified Beer Injury; U.D.I., Unidentified Drinking Injury.

Party Foul • An incident that goes against the rules of the party. For example, spilling your glass of red wine on the Dean's white carpet during an elegant mixer. *See page 156.*

Pass Back • When you sneak your I.D. back to your friends so they can get into the same bar using the same I.D.

Penalty Box • The area behind the back seat of a sport utility vehicle usually accommodates the sixth passenger who needs a ride home after a night of drinking.

Permadrunk • When someone is always acting stupid, even when sober.

Pissing Clear • The point at which one has consumed enough alcohol to turn one's urine transparent. Signfies the beginning of a buzz.

Plead the Fifth • Somewhat unrelated to the amendment in the Constitution; exercising your right to remain silent because you consumed about a fifth and cannot recall the bulk of the previous evening's events.

P.O.M.A. (Pee Out My Ass) • After a night of heavy drinking you could swear it was pee coming out of your butt. *See also AIDS.*

Pre (short for Pre-drinking or Pre-gaming) • The practice of drinking prior to going out. "Wanna pre before the bar?" *A.k.a. Front Loading.*

Puff Puff Give • The proper procedure to follow when smoking a joint in a group. Two puffs then pass the joint. Anyone who doesn't follow that rule deserves to get punched. *A.k.a. Puff Puff Pass.*

Pull Tubes • Take drags from a bong. *See also Snap.*

Rager • A massive wild party.

Roll or Bowl • Pot-smoker's dilemma, whether to roll a joint or indulge in the less strenuous packing of a bowl (for a pipe or bong).

Sausage Fest • A party with way more males than females. *A.k.a. Sausage Party, Sword Fight.*

Sentinels • People at a party who don't live there, yet patrol the party cracking down on misbehaviors anyway.

Sexile • The act of one roommate booting the other roommate out of their shared room for the express purpose of hooking up. Often requested with a sock on the doorknob.

Shakes • The tremors that result from drinking way too much.

Shoot the Boot • Rugby term for a penalty for a party foul. The offender removes his shoe and passes it around. Beer is poured in and then dirt, spit, etc. Offender must then "shoot the boot," i.e., chug the beer from the shoe. Usually accompanied by the chant "Oh ah, shoot that boot!"

Shotgun • 1) To pound a beer by puncturing the side of the can and opening the top to make the beer spurt out in a powerful stream; 2) the passenger seat in an automobile that must be claimed by an eponymous proclamation. In other words, you got to call, "Shotgun!" to ride shotgun.

Silver-Tongued • Drunk to the point of slurring your speech.

Skull • To down the contents of whatever beverage you're currently drinking. *A.k.a. Chug.*

Snap • To smoke a bong bowl in one toke—no passin'.

Snarf • The act of spewing your drink out of your nose, usually from poorly timed laughter.

Sneaky Drunk • An individual who, when drunk, has an increased sense of stealth and cunning. Often suffers from delusions of invisibility.

Spaulding • A half-full, discarded drink. Named in loving tribute to the character in *Caddyshack*.

Spins • This is when you are so drunk that it feels like the room won't stop spinning.

Splattened • Getting splattered (really, really drunk) and flattened (verbally beat up by your BF/GF) in the same night.

Suicide Break • To go outside to smoke a butt.

Surfacing • When you pull yourself out of a stupor long enough to realize what exactly is going on.

Talking to Bob (Marley) • Someone who is smoking alone in their room. "Where's Joe?" "Oh. He's just talking to Bob."

T.A.T. (Talk After Toke) • This is what you say to that chatty friend in the circle when they won't shut up and pass it.

T.D.I. (Trivial Drinking Injuries) • Most drinking injuries fall under this category. These are the cuts, bruises, scratches, and sprains that just kind of hurt, but you ignore until the pain goes away a couple of days later. May or may not be a MDA.

Ten-Second Rule • Drunk version of the Three-Second Rule. Refers to how long food can be on the ground before it is no longer "safe" to eat.

That Guy • An individual one does not wish to become. Often one's drunken persona who decides things like exposing oneself in public or taunting cops are good ideas. *A.k.a. Turd Ferguson.*

The Stupids • What you have the day after a night of hard drinking, and you well think not straight good.

Tomb of the Dead Soldiers • A trash can filled with many, many beer cans. Sometimes brings a tear to the eye.

Travelers • Alcohol you take with you on the way to events, bars, and parties. *A.k.a. Road Beers, Roadies.*

Trifecta • The act of frequenting and drinking at three different bars in one night.

Triple Threat • A party with multiple vices, such as beer being one threat, marijuana being a second, and hook-ups being a third.

Turn-Around • The amount of time from the last drink on one day to the first drink on the next.

Undie Bongs • An early morning smoke-up session. *See Kegs and Eggs.*

Vat • An alcoholic beverage that tastes like fruit punch, consisting of various forms of alcohol and fruit juices. It gets its name from the fact that it's often made in large quantities and served out of large containers or "vats." *A.k.a. Grain Punch, Hunch Punch, Jungle Juice, Trash Can.*

Wake and Bake • The habit of starting one's morning with a toke.

Walking Dead • Someone who passes out for thirty minutes or so, wakes up, and attempts to rejoin the party!

Whirlies • It's that lightheaded-spinning, ball-of-ice-in-your-stomach feeling that you get immediately before booting.

W.M.D. ("We Must Depart!") •
A command code used for
immediate withdrawal of your
posse from a party, usually
because of one of your posse is
doing something that will get
your collective ass kicked.

Wounded Soldier • A full beer
found when cleaning up the next
day after a party.
A.k.a. Larry.

YOLO (You Only Live Once) •
A rally cry for Gen Y Party
Animals in the year 2011 when
hip-hop artist Drake popularized
it in his song "The Motto," and as
a hashtag on Twitter. For example,
"Gonna try to touch this cop's gun,
lol #YOLO."

Zamboni • A roll of paper towels
or toilet paper used to mop up
spilled fluids. Particularly helpful
during drinking games.

Zeech • As a result of drinking/
smoking too much, a person
acquires zombie and leechlike
characteristics such as they
can't respond to their own name,
and cling on to you in order
to keep their balance.

How to Retell a Killer Story

A PARTY ANIMAL NEEDS TO BE ABLE TO DO MORE than just keg
stands and beer bongs. If he wants to keep his audience truly engaged,
he also has to know how to tell a killer party story. Lend us your ears as
we teach you how to become an expert spinner of yarns.

1. CUT TO THE CHASE

A good story should never, ever be told in real time. Establish the
context of your tale quickly and then jump to the heart of the action.

THE BOOK OF THE PARTY ANIMAL

2. USE PROPS

Does your story involve gunfire? Try using a roman candle to retell it. Were you caught in a torrential rain pour? Turn on the garden hose to illustrate the effect. Props have the potential to transform a tired old chestnut into a tale of epic proportions.

3. USE ACCENTS

The easiest way of differentiating characters in your story is to assign each one a unique accent. This technique is especially effective with jokes and other short tales that rely upon instantly recognizable stereotypes.

4. EXAGGERATE

Unlike essays, party stories don't require dozens of sources and annotations, so feel free to play fast and loose with the details in order to help enhance the plot. In general, any measurement can reasonably be exaggerated by two inches, any weight by 50 lbs., and any conquest by two cup sizes.

5. TAKE A PAGE OUT OF HEMINGWAY'S PLAYBOOK

The key to a great story isn't in what you tell, but in what you leave out. Follow the lead of Ernest Hemingway, who believed that a good story should be like an iceberg with nine-tenths of the action happening beneath the surface.

6. BETTER STORIES COME FROM BETTER TIMES

We invite you to preserve the traditions of the North American Party Animal by putting down this book, picking up a cold one, gathering your posse and rocking out. Party on, future Party Animal, party on.

Acknowledgments

The authors would like to thank Kurt Angle, Chris Barish, David Grubb, Mike Krilivsky, David Lamm, Marty Lang, Elise McDonough, Noel Nickol, Derrick Pittman, Mike Student, and Ravin' Dave for sharing their animal expertise.

We would also like to thank the entire team at Chronicle Books, especially Emily Haynes and Sarah Malarkey for making partying their business, and our friends at Levine Greenberg, especially Stephanie Kip Rostan and Monika Verma for representing partying, literally, and to all our fellow Party Animals the world over for partying like there's no tomorrow.

Dan would like to personally thank all the great animals he has had the pleasure to party with including but not limited to: The Original Pit Crew, The Wildcats, The O.B.C, The Calabria Gang, The Colt-Jefferson Posse, The Jungle (R.I.P), The Celeron Zoo, The Hunting Lodge, The Hilltoppers, and The BOMBED Army. And a special rally cry goes out to my beautiful and amazing wife for her unconditional love and support in all my punkish pursuits.

Ben would like to personally thank all of the great Party Animals he has met: from suburbs of PGH to the Quad of WFU, from the bars and bushes of Atlanta to the backyards of Connecticut. A shout out to the Moon Pi's—I hope this is required reading. And a special classy Cheers to the best partner any Animal could ask for: my wife.